Anne's glory box

Gloria McKinnon

Contents

Editorial
Managing Editor: Judy Poulos
Editorial Assistant: Ella Martin
Editorial Coordinator: Margaret Kelly

Photography
Andrew Elton

Styling
Lisa Hilton

Illustrations
Lesley Griffith

Design and Production
Managers: Sheridan Carter, Anna Maguire
Design: Jenny Pace
Layout: Lulu Dougherty

Published by J.B. Fairfax Press Pty Limited
80-82 McLachlan Ave
Rushcutters Bay, NSW 2011, Australia
A.C.N. 003 738 430
Formatted by J.B. Fairfax Press Pty Limited
Printed by Toppan Printing Company, Hong Kong

JBFP 366

ANNE'S GLORY BOX
Series ISBN 1 86343 166 7
Book 4 ISBN 1 86343 202 7

Travelling with Anne's Glory Box

I consider myself fortunate to have a career that I enjoy. People tell me I'm lucky to own Anne's Glory Box – that isn't due to luck, but to hard work. I'm really lucky because of the interesting people I meet and the places I get to visit.

I meet wonderful students from whom I learn so much. What I learn is not always needlework, but things like 'how to manage a husband' – especially when you buy more fabric and he thinks you have enough! Mary Ellen Hopkins has inspired us to make a wallhanging for just such occasions. It says: 'My husband says if I buy any more fabric, he will leave me. I will miss him terribly.'

I have met students who keep fabric in the boot of the car, in an old freezer in the garage or even in the ceiling. And, of course, stitchers like us do the same with threads, ribbons, books and patterns.

Travelling to the United States is a great pleasure. I teach many classes there, and it has become like a second home to me. I love the enthusiasm of my American students and their desire for anything Australian. Recently, I taught silk ribbon embroidery in a three-day retreat at Big Bear in California. The students came from Los Angeles where they don't see the stars at night because of the smog, so at night we walked up the hill and looked at the stars as though we were observing a miracle! Oh, the things we take for granted.

It was also in California that I learned about cloth dolly clubs and attended quite a few meetings. We have now started our own cloth dolly club at the store, the first one in Australia. On the back cover of this book, you will see the happy faces and creativity of one of the meetings.

New Zealand is another country that I keep going back to because of the friendships that have developed over the years. I have some wonderful memories, including judging a teddy bear competition in Auckland until three in the morning, then going to sleep under the table. When I awoke, I found that the bears I had judged the night before and left on the table were now living on an island. While I slept, someone had transformed the stage into a rocky shoreline complete with yacht! The bears were sunbaking, picnicking, up the mast and generally having a great time.

CHAIR FROM CANE & COTTAGE, LINDFIELD, NSW

Teaching at the Martha Pullen School of Art Fashion in Huntsville, Alabama, is particularly interesting. Because the students come from all over the globe, it's a wonderful opportunity to meet fellow stitchers from faraway places.

Such visits also give me the opportunity to meet people I have been reading about for years, such as the friends at McCalls Needlework in Alabama, whose magazine I have been buying for thirty years. It was great to meet them in person.

Gloria

Double Wedding Ring Quilt

STITCHED BY YAN PRING WITH THANKS TO JOHN FLYNN

This quilt pattern has been a favourite of quilters for a very long time. Now, thanks to John's strip-piecing method and special techniques, you can make this quilt more easily than ever before.

You can purchase John's Double Wedding Ring Template Set or you can make your own from the ones we have provided on the pattern sheet.

As there are two colour gradings in this quilt (blue and pink), you will need twelve different fabrics for the arcs, six in each grading. For the corners, you will need two colour combinations, a light and a dark to suit each colour grading from the arcs (four fabrics). Fat quarters are the ideal way to buy all these fabrics.

Finished size: 108 cm (42.5 in) square

Materials

- **1.1 m (1^1/8 yd) of background fabric**
- **fat quarters for the arcs and corners**
- **1.25 m (1^1/3 yd) of fabric for the backing**
- **1.25 m (1^1/3 yd) of wadding**
- **75 cm (30 in) of fabric for the binding**
- **coloured pencils**
- **cutting mat**
- **rotary cutter**
- **ruler**
- **matching sewing thread**
- **quilting thread**
- **template plastic**
- **black fineline permanent marker pen**

Method

See the Templates on the Pull Out Pattern Sheet and the Quilt Diagram on page 7.

Preparation

1 For this quilt it is very important that your seam allowances are extremely accurate. To ensure this, make two seam marks on the plate of your sewing machine – one at 6 mm (^{1}/4 in) and another one at 12 mm (^{1}/2 in) for the arc seam adjustment.

2 With the coloured pencils, colour in the quilt diagram on page 7, according to your chosen fabrics, so you can use it for reference.

3 Arrange the fabrics in the order in which you have decided to use them.

For the arcs

4 Cut 5.5 cm (2^1/4 in) wide strips of six fabrics for each colour grading. Strip-piece the strips into panels. Press all the seams in the same direction. Check the width of each fabric strip in the panel. Each one should be exactly 4.5 cm (1^3/4 in) wide. If they are not, you have not kept a correct seam allowance and you will need to unpick and do it again.

5 Straighten one edge of the panel, then cut it into 6.4 cm (2^1/2 in) wide strips. You will need twenty-four of each colour grading.

6 This step is extremely important: it holds the secret of success for this quilt. Having decided on your colour gradings, divide your two bundles of strips into halves so that one half has the lighter fabrics at one end and the other half has the reverse. Fold back the first fabric on the strip and resew the seam, starting at 6 mm (^{1}/4 in) and increasing to that extra 6 mm (^{1}/4 in) you have marked on the plate of your sewing machine (Fig. 1). Resew each seam for the arc in the same way. Place the arc on the ironing board and, with the inside curve of the arc facing you, press all the seams to the left. Before you go any further, check the curve of your arc with the arc template. If your curve is not as sharp as the template, pull the arc to fit and trim the ends. If your curve is too sharp and your arc is too short, you have increased your seams too much and will have to try again. If your arc fits well, sew all your other arcs in the same way.

Piecing

1 Using the templates, cut forty-eight melons and nine centres from the background fabric.

2 Set half of each arc group aside. Sew the other half to the melons in the following way. Mark the centre of the melon by finger-creasing it into quarters. Pin the centre to the centre seam of the arc (Fig. 2). Matching the ends of the arc to the edges of the melon, pin the edges together with the right sides facing. Stitch, pulling the fabric gently to shape it as you go (Fig. 3).

3 Cut the corner fabrics into squares for the four-patches, using the template. For this quilt you need sixteen of each of the four fabrics.

4 Stitch squares of one fabric to each end of half of the remaining melons, then attach the second colour to each end of the rest. Do the same for the other colour combination. Attach this lengthened arc to the arc-melon units, gently adjusting the shape as you go.

5 It is now time to lay out your quilt so all the pieces can be assembled, using your coloured quilt diagram as a guide. Finger-crease the centre piece along the centre line marked on the pattern. Pin the middle seam of the arc-melon unit to this line. Pin the ends of the centre piece to the arc-melon unit so that the end extends 6 mm (1/4 in) past the seam between the arc and the four-patch piece. Use a pin to mark the seam. Turn the seam towards the arc where possible. Stitch the units.

6 By alternating blocks, you will be able to assemble the rows of the quilt so that the edges are one continuous curved line (Fig. 4). First pin each row, then sew the entire seam. You will have three rows of three blocks.

7 Sew the rows together, then sew on the appropriate arc-melon units around the edge to complete the top. For the complete four-patch units around the edges and to avoid set-in corners, it is best to sew them to the arc-melon units before the arc-melon units are joined to the rows.

Quilting

Place the backing fabric face down with the wadding on top. Place the quilt top on top of that, face up. Baste the layers of the quilt together horizontally, vertically and diagonally. Quilt in the plain areas, either by hand or machine.

Binding

Because the quilt has curved edges, cut 7 cm (2 3/4 in) wide bias strips for binding. Trim the wadding and the backing to the size and shape of the quilt top. Fold the binding over double, with the wrong sides facing. Sew the binding to the quilt, with the right sides facing and the raw edges even. Turn the folded edge of the binding to the back of the quilt and slipstitch it into place.

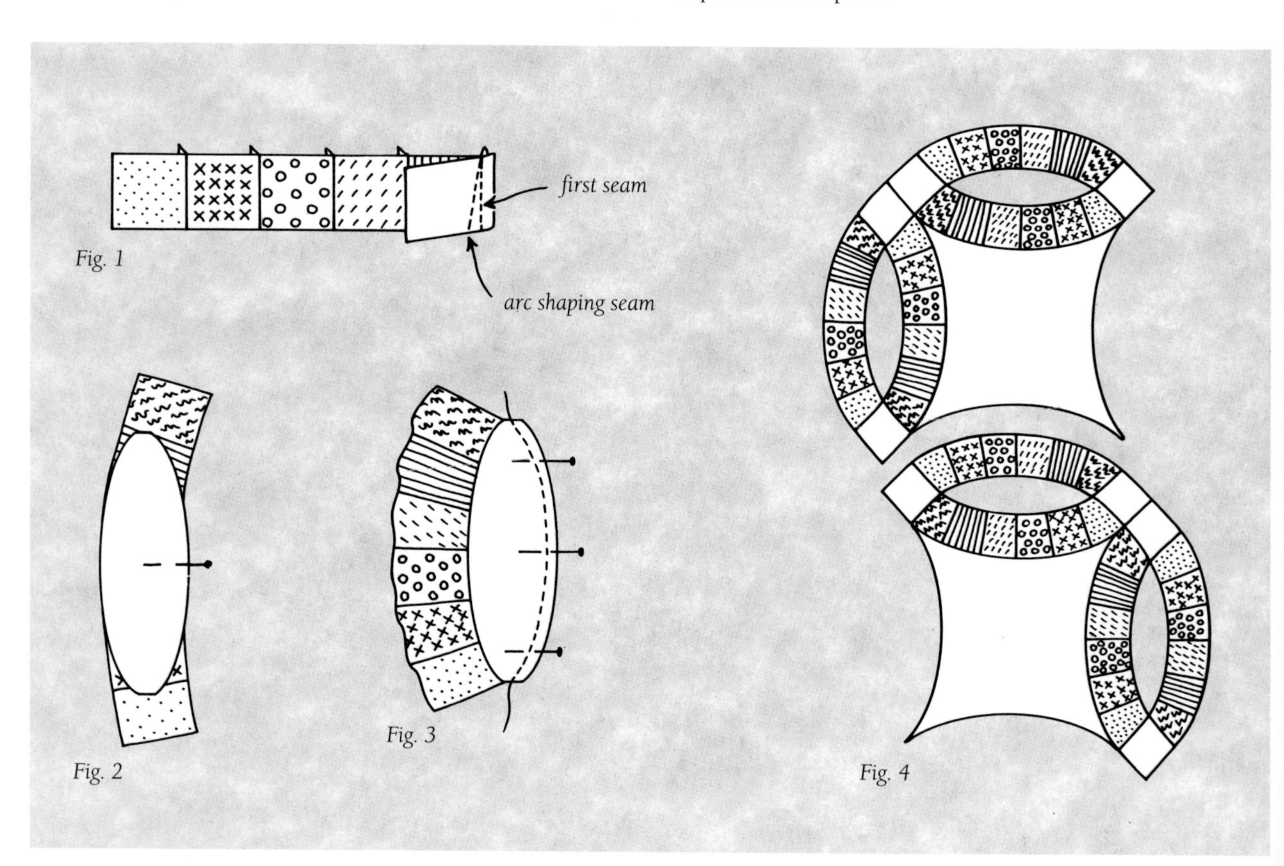

Fig. 1

Fig. 2

Fig. 3

Fig. 4

Quilt Diagram

Nostalgia Box

MADE BY GLORIA MCKINNON

What better way to preserve your special keepsakes than with this lovely box.

Materials

- wooden nostalgia box, frame and mat
- acrylic paint for the base coat
- paintbrush
- glue gun
- antiquing medium (optional)
- oil paint, Burnt Umber (optional)
- soft cloth
- antique laces
- assorted memorabilia: postcards, photographs, small teddy bears, dolls, trinkets, dried flowers, ribbons, locks of hair, lockets and so on

Note: You can seal your box by means of a glass front, fixed under the frame.

Method

1 Paint the inside and outside of the box with two coats of acrylic paint, allowing the paint to dry thoroughly between coats. Paint the frame in the same way as the box.

2 If you wish to antique the frame, gently rub a little of the Burnt Umber oil paint and the antiquing medium on the frame, using the soft cloth. Allow it to dry for five minutes, then, with a circular motion, wipe off the frame until you have an antique finish that you like.

3 Attach the lace background to the inside back of the box, using the glue gun. Arrange all the trinkets and memorabilia on the background and on the 'floor' of the box, beginning with the larger items and filling in with the smaller ones. To ensure that there are no blank spots, view the arrangement from all angles, then glue all the items in place.

4 To give added depth to the box, glue a piece of lace across the front of the mat at the top.

5 When you are happy with the arrangement, fix the frame into place across the front of the box.

HAT FROM SANDY DE BEYER, MOSMAN, NSW. HAT STAND, BABIES TEETHING RING AND CARD FROM MOSMAN ANTIQUE CENTRE, MOSMAN, NSW. SILVER HEART BOX FROM HOME & GARDEN ON THE MALL, SKYGARDENS, NSW

Christening Gown Pillowcase

MADE BY WENDY LEE RAGAN WITH THANKS TO MARGARET BOYLES

This beautiful lace-trimmed pillowcase is definitely a family heirloom in the making.

Fits a pillow: 51 cm (20 in) wide

Materials

- **1 m ($1^1/_8$ yd) of linen or Swiss batiste**
- **4.75 m ($5^1/_4$ yd) of lace (linen) tape, pale pink**
- **3 m ($3^1/_4$ yd) of lace insertion, number 1**
- **2 m ($2^1/_4$ yd) of lace insertion, number 2**
- **2.1 m ($2^1/_3$ yd) of lace insertion, number 3 (optional)**
- **4.8 m ($5^1/_3$ yd) of lace edging**
- **2.4 m ($2^2/_3$ yd) of entredeux**
- **Floche embroidery thread in your chosen colours for the flower embroidery**
- **Piecemaker between needles, size 7**
- **Madeira Tanne cotton thread, no. 80, white**
- **ribbon for the beading and the eyelets**
- **spray starch**
- **water-soluble marker pen OR an HB, 2H or 3H pencil**

For the optional flounced inner pillowcase

- **1 m ($1^1/_8$ yd) of Swiss batiste, white**
- **1 m ($1^1/_8$ yd) of Swiss batiste, pale pink**
- **4.5 m (5 yd) of lace edging**
- **1.2 m ($1^1/_3$ yd) of 4 cm ($1^1/_2$ in) wide Swiss beading**

Method

See the Pattern, Embroidery Design and Monogram on the Pull Out Pattern Sheet and on page 13.

1 Pull threads on the edges of the linen to even them off. Spray the linen with starch and press it well.

2 Trace the oval embroidery design from page 13 and the monogram from the pattern sheet onto the linen. Embroider the design in the stitches indicated, following the stitch guide on page 12. Do not embroider the feather stitch until after the lace and tape are pinstitched into place. Using a stiletto or something similar, make the two small eyelet holes in the oval. Stitch around the holes with fine buttonhole stitches. When the embroidery is completed, press the linen again, using a well-padded ironing board and a pressing cloth.

3 Curve, shape and mitre the lace tape, then baste it into place by hand as indicated on the pattern.

4 Baste by hand as many rows of the optional lace insertions as you wish. Carefully spray the piece with starch and press again with a medium iron setting.

5 Pinstitch the lace and tape into place. Work the feather stitch embroidery. When all the lace is applied and the embroidery completed, cut away the linen from behind the lace insertion, but not from behind the lace tape.

6 Join the side seam of the pillowcase, using a French seam. Sew the top of the pillowcase with a French seam.

7 Attach the entredeux to the scallops and points on the bottom edge of the pillowcase.

8 Carefully wash the pillowcase to remove all marker pen or pencil marks, then press it while it is still slightly damp, using the padded ironing board and the pressing cloth.

9 Gather the lace edging and stitch it to the entredeux at the bottom of the pillowcase. Roll and whip the raw edge of the lace edging. Insert the ribbon.

For the flounced inner pillowcase

1 Repeat step 1 for the pillowcase. Fold the batiste over double, then join the sides and one end with French seams, leaving one end open. Attach Swiss beading to the open end of the pillowcase.

2 On the pale pink Swiss batiste, pull threads to even the edges, then cut two pieces, each approximately 46 cm x 112 cm (18 in x 44 in). Join them with a French seam to form a piece approximately 46 cm x 224 cm (18 in x 88 in).

3 Draw scallops along one long edge of the pink batiste. Shape and baste the lace edging along the scallops. French seam the short ends closed, forming a loop. Pinstitch the lace edging to the pink batiste. Cut away the fabric from behind the lace edging.

4 At the straight end of the pink batiste, run three rows of gathering thread, using a regular stitch length. Pull up the gathering to fit the Swiss beading on the end of the pillowcase. Pin, then stitch the gathered edge to the beading. Run ribbon through the beading. Press the pillowcase and flounce carefully.

BEDHEAD FROM TONBRIDGE ANTIQUES, ROSEVILLE, NSW. BEDLINEN FROM BED BATH N' TABLE, SKYGARDENS, NSW. FABRIC FLOWERS FROM SANDY DE BEYER, MOSMAN, NSW

Stitch Guide

Shadow embroidery

Use a crewel needle, size 10, and a 45 cm/18 in single strand of stranded embroidery cotton. Place the fabric in a hoop and begin with a waste knot. In shadow stitch, you form a basketweave of thread that covers the area to be filled and is surrounded by back stitches.

1 Bring the needle through at **a** and take a stitch to **b**. Bring the needle up at **c** and take a stitch to **b**. (Fig. A)

2 Bring the needle up at **d** and take a stitch to **a**. On the wrong side, carry the thread over, bringing it out at **e** and take a stitch to **c**. (Fig. B)

3 On the wrong side, carry the thread over, bringing it out at **f** then take a stitch back to **d**. On the wrong side, carry the thread over, bringing it out at **g** then take a stitch back to **e**. Continue in this way until the area is filled. (Fig. C)

Granitos or rondels

These are tiny dots made by laying six or seven straight stitches over one another. They can be worked with or without a hoop.

Split stitch

This is commonly used for padding which is covered by other stitches. It can be worked with or without a hoop. (Fig. D)

Bullion stitches

Bullion stitches are the basis for many flowers.

1 Begin by anchoring the thread, then take a stitch from **a** to **b**, taking the needle back to **a**. Insert the needle at **b** again, just up to the eye. (Fig. E)

2 Wrap the thread around the needle, keeping it close to **a** (Fig. F). Controlling the wraps firmly with your left thumb, push the needle through and slide the wraps off the needle. Slide the wraps down the thread until they are lying on the fabric. Reinsert the needle at **b**.

Bullion rosebuds are made by laying two bullion stitches side by side. Make one of the bullions one wrap larger than the other.

For a bullion rose, make three bullions side by side. The inside one is usually one or two wraps smaller than the outside ones. Here's a tip: wrap the thread around the needle until the tube is the desired length, then add one more wrap. This is to compensate for the fact that the bullion will compact when you slide it off the needle.
For bullion pinwheels, draw a circle of the desired size with a dot in the centre. Stitch around the outside with split stitches, then make bullions from the outside ring, over the split stitches, into the centre, until the circle is filled.

Shaded eyelets

1 Draw an oval with an offset circle inside it. Outline both with split stitches (Fig. G). With an awl, push open the threads inside the circle. Don't break the threads.

2 Inside the oval, stitch two or three layers of padding satin stitches, alternating the direction of the layers. (Fig. H)

3 When the padding is completed, satin stitch around the eyelet over the padding (Fig. J). These shaded eyelets can be stitched with or without a hoop.

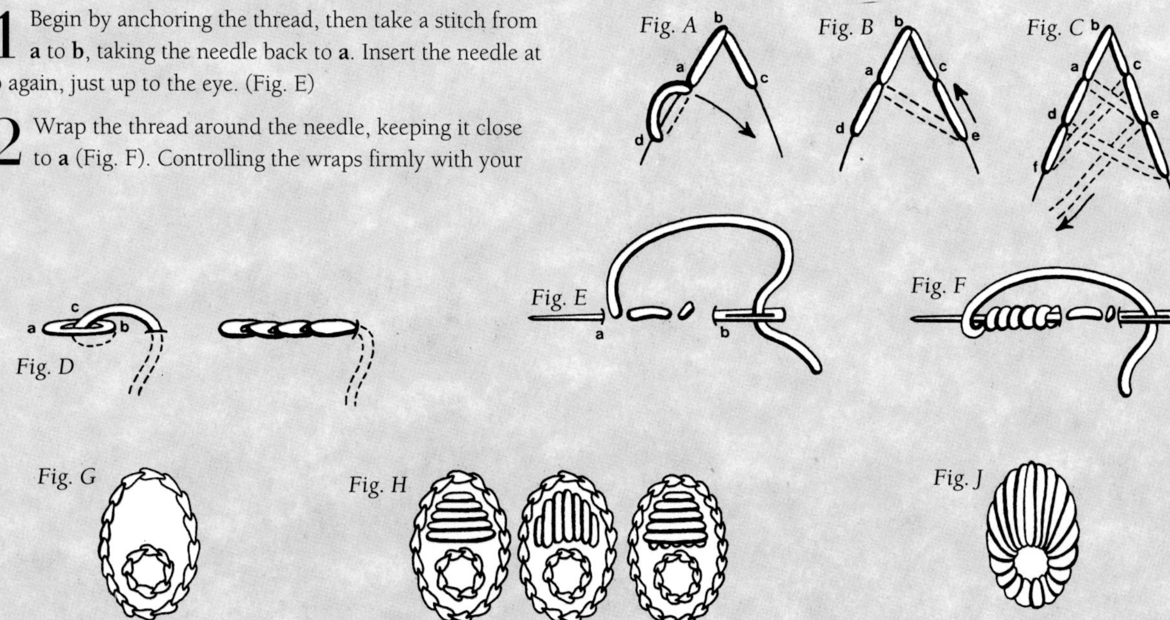

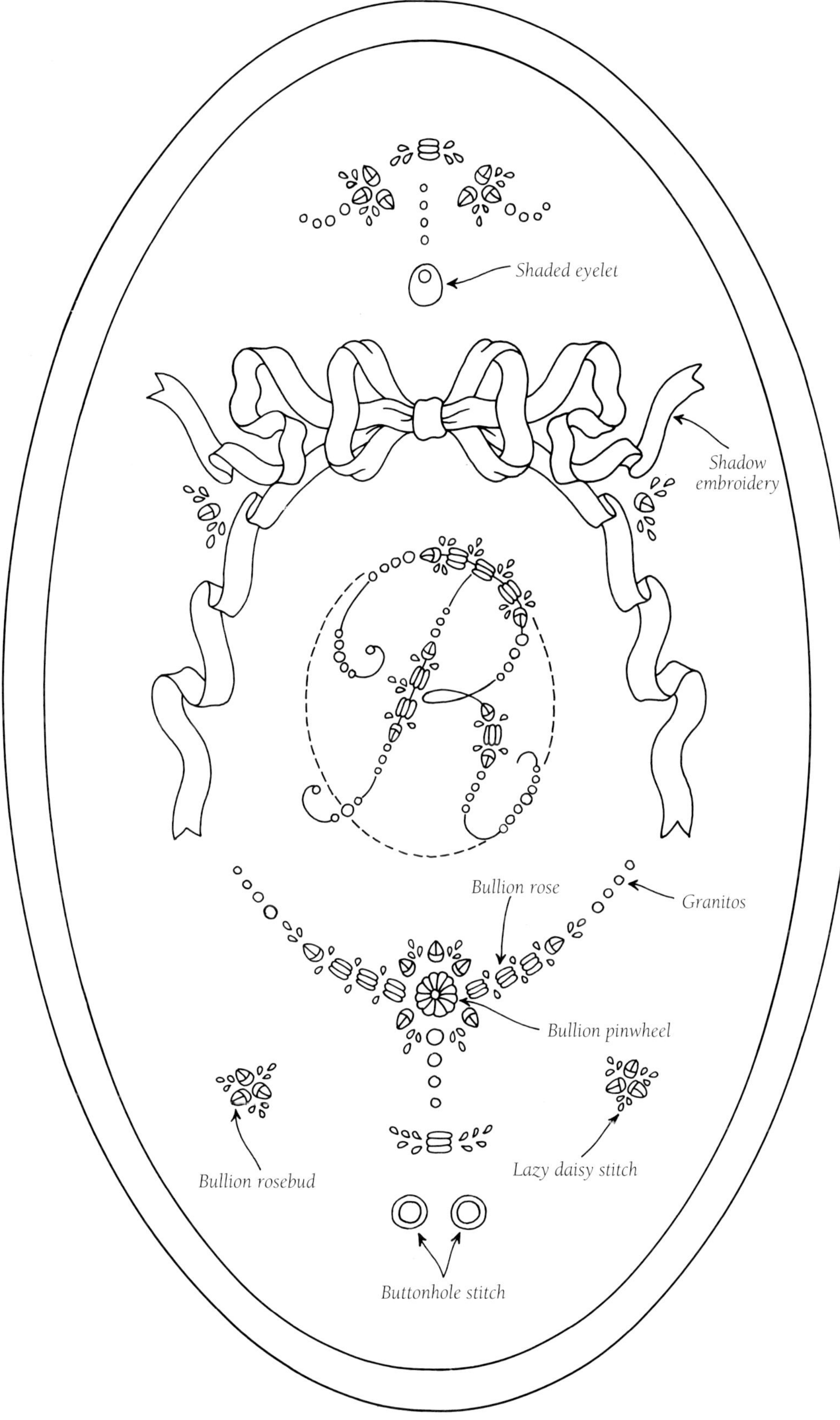
Shaded eyelet
Shadow embroidery
Bullion rose
Granitos
Bullion pinwheel
Bullion rosebud
Lazy daisy stitch
Buttonhole stitch

Spring Blossoms

STITCHED BY CAROLINE PEARCE

Thanks to the wonderful talents of wool artist, Merilyn Ann Whalan, these blossoms are so realistic, you feel you can pick them right off the wall.

Materials

- **50 cm (19½ in) square of linen**
- **tracing paper**
- **pencil**
- **blue water-soluble marker pen**
- **Piecemaker chenille needle, size 22**
- **Piecemaker large tapestry needle**
- **Mill Hill beads Col. 02024**
- **Appleton's Crewel Wool: Pinks 755, 753, 143; Apricot 705; Lavender 602; Jacaranda 891, Blue 892; Yellow 851; Greens 292, 334**
- **Strand Embroidery Yarn, 113 OR Appleton's Crewel Wool, 894**
- **DMC Medici: Greens 8406, 8407**
- **Fancyworks 2 ply yarn: Avocado, Peach, Dusk**
- **Littlewood Fleece Yarns Gossamer Mohair: Claret 17, Green 6, Yellow 25**
- **Madeira silk thread: 1912, 2114, 1703, Black**
- **Madeira Decora, 1557**
- **Kanagawa Buttonhole Twist: 827, 114**
- **Waterlilies Silk 12 ply, Olive**
- **Mary Hart Davies overdyed silk, 3B**
- **DMC stranded cotton, 3721**
- **Minnamurra Stranded Cotton, 110**

Method

See the Embroidery Design on the Pull Out Pattern Sheet.

Preparation

1 Overcast or zigzag the edges of the linen to prevent them fraying.

2 Trace the embroidery design, marking the centre of the flowers and positions of the buds on the tracing. Punch a hole through the centre of each flower with a large tapestry needle and, through the hole, mark these points on the linen with the water-soluble pen. Do not transfer any more of the design to the linen at this point. Once the flowers are embroidered, draw on the stems, work the buds and leaves and the small three-petalled flowers. Finally, add the tendrils.

For the flowers

1 Each flower is composed of five petals. Using the chenille needle and the colours indicated in the chart on page 17, work three petals in the shape of a Y, then fill in the last two petals, leaving quite a large space in the centre to allow for six or seven French knots. Each petal is approximately 1 cm (3/8 in) long and is made up of about seven stitches into the same holes, at the top and bottom of the petal. Place the stitches, alternately, to the right, then to the left of the first stitch. Do this by ensuring the threads are to the left of the needle for the stitch to sit on the left and to the right of the needle for the stitch to sit on the right (Figs 1 and 2). It is important to put your needle under each stitch as you pull the threads through so that the strands lie parallel and are not too tight. Space each petal so that it just touches the adjacent petal for about 3 mm (1/8 in) at the centre.

2 Work all five petals, then, using a strand of Fancyworks Avocado, work a straight stitch in between each petal, from the centre out to where the petals just separate. Tip and outline each petal with a straight stitch and a fly stitch. (Fig. 3)

3 Fill the centres of the large flowers with about seven French knots of three wraps each. Work three French knots in the centres of the periwinkles and the three-petalled yellow flowers. When you have finished the centres of the large flowers, work three straight stitches in silk on each petal beginning in the centre of the petal and converging at the centre of the flower. (Fig. 4)

4 Work the small flowers in the same way as the large ones, using a smaller initial stitch and fewer stitches in each petal. Separate the petals on the periwinkle by a straight stitch in the same colour as you used to tip the petals.

For the buds

Work the buds in the same way as the flower petals. You can vary the size of the buds by altering the length of the stitch and/or the number of stitches. First, couch the stem in place with one strand of green. Leave the thread on the right side of

the work, out of the way. Work the petal part of the bud, then add two or three straight stitches around the petal in green, working one small stitch in the centre. Work five or six small stitches in green at the base of the bud as for the petals (Fig. 5). To give extra depth to the bud, add some straight stitches in the green silk over the green wool stitches. For the base of the bud, work fly stitches with a long anchor stitch extending beyond the point of the bud. (Fig. 6)

For the leaves

1 Using the chenille needle and a single strand of Gossamer Mohair, couch the stems in place.

2 Starting at the tip of the leaf, work the leaves in fly stitch. To do this successfully, take a very uneven initial fly stitch that is quite closed. Do not anchor the stitch too close. Keep the anchor stitch fairly long so that the leaf has a nice deep V shape. If the fly stitch is too short and too open, the leaves will look like a fishbone fern. The anchor stitches make the mid rib of the leaf. If you want your leaf to curl to the right, make an uneven fly stitch so that the left side of the stitch is much longer than the right (Fig. 7); reverse this for a leaf that curls to the left.

3 To finish the leaf, come up 2 mm (1/16 in) away from the base of the leaf and slide the needle under the last stitch, working from right to left, and make a smocker's knot. Anchor the knot by returning the thread to the back of the work through the stem.

For the tendrils and stems

1 Draw in some interesting lines on the linen with the water-soluble pen. Using a single strand of crewel, Medici or silk, secure the thread at the back of the work, come out on the right side of the work and lay the thread along the line, pinning it where necessary. Work tiny stitches across the thread, coming up and going down into the same hole, to secure the stem.

2 Whip the stem by going over and over the thread without piercing the fabric. Use tiny fly stitches along the stem for the thorns.

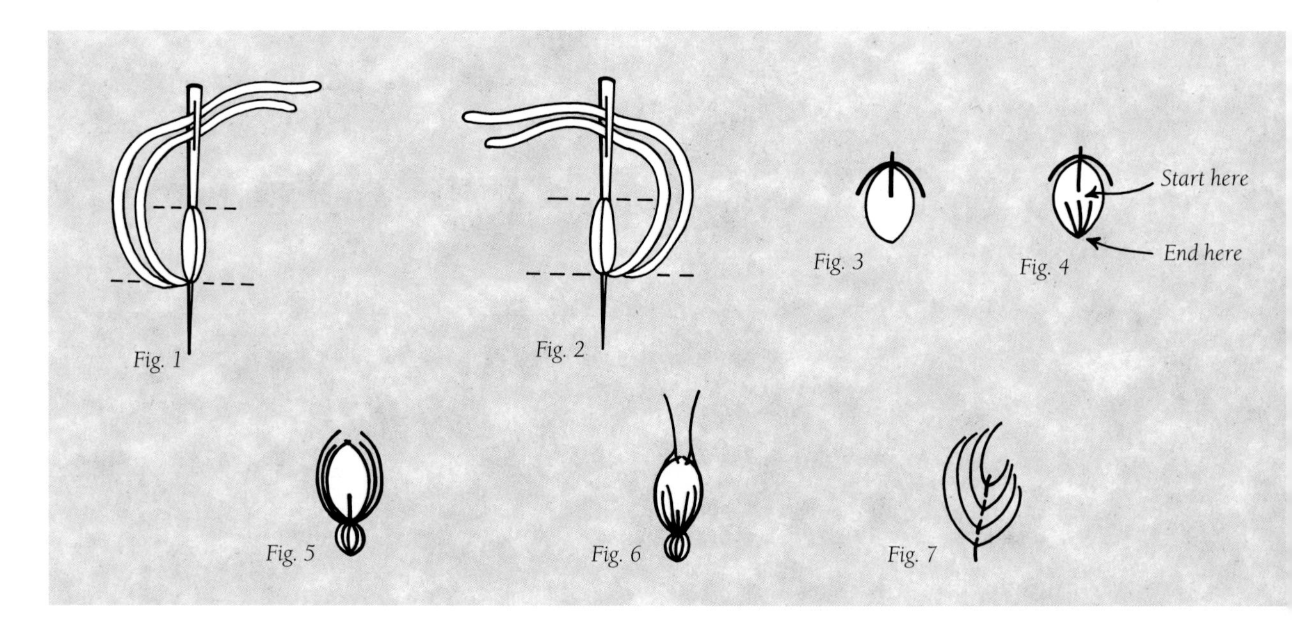

Fig. 1 Fig. 2 Fig. 3 Fig. 4 Fig. 5 Fig. 6 Fig. 7

Wool Thread Chart

FLOWER	PETAL	TIPPING	CENTRE	3 STRAIGHT STITCHES
1	2 strands Gossamer Mohair Claret	1 strand Mary Hart Davies 3B	1 strand Gossamer Mohair 25 plus 1 strand Black Madeira silk	1 strand Kanagawa 114
2	2 strands Fancyworks, Dusk	1 strand Appleton's 755	as above	as above
3	1 strand each of Appleton's 755 & 143	1 strand Appleton's 602	as above Finally, stitch on beads with matching thread	
4	2 strands Appleton's 753	1 strand Appleton's 143	4 knots of the above combination & 3 knots of Fancyworks Avocado & 1 strand Madeira 2114	1 strand Decora 1557
5	2 strands Fancyworks, Peach	1 strand of the deep section of Fancyworks, Peach	as above	as above
6	2 strands Appleton's 705	1 strand Fancyworks, Peach	as above	as above
Periwinkle 7	2 strands Appleton's 891	1 strand Appleton's 892	1 strand Appleton's 851 & 1 strand Madeira 2114	
8	2 strands Appleton's 892	1 strand Strand 113	as above	
3-petalled flowers	2 strands Appleton's 851	2 strands Minnamurra 110	1 strand Kanagawa 827 & 2 strands DMC 3721	
BUD				
A	2 strands Fancyworks, Dusk	1 strand Appleton's 334		
B	2 strands Fancyworks, Dusk	1 strand Appleton's 292		
C	2 strands Fancyworks, Peach	1 strand Appleton's 292		
D	1 strand each of Fancyworks, Peach & Appleton's 705	1 strand Medici 8407, stem is whipped with Madeira 1703		
E	as above	1 strand Medici 8406, stem is whipped with Waterlilies, Olive		
F	2 strands Appleton's 705	1 strand Appleton's 334 around the bud, stem is whipped with Waterlilies, Olive		
G	2 strands Appleton's 891	1 strand Appleton's 892, stem is 1 strand Medici 8406		

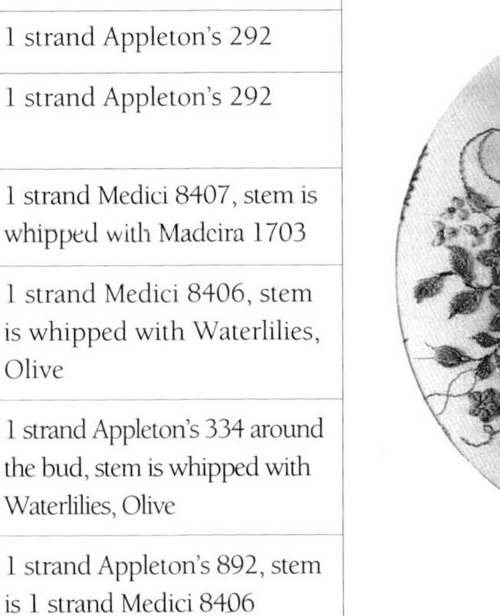

Velvet-covered Coathanger

MADE BY FAY KING

This splendid coathanger would make the perfect gift for a bride, or for a friend 'who has everything'.

Materials

- wooden coathanger
- 50 cm (20 in) of cotton velvet or velveteen
- 1 m (40 in) of 12 mm (1/2 in) wide rayon ribbon in each of four colours
- 2.2 m (2 1/4 yd) of green silk ribbon
- strips of wadding for wrapping the coathanger
- 50 cm (20 in) of Pellon
- thread to match the rayon ribbons
- 1 m (40 in) of cord to match the velvet or velveteen
- Piecemaker crewel needle, size 9
- Piecemaker tapestry needle, size 22
- Piecemaker straw needle, size 8
- Madeira silk thread, Ecru
- Mill Hill beads to match the ribbons
- 35 cm (14 in) of 7 mm (5/16 in) wide ribbon to match the velvet or velveteen
- sewing thread to match the velvet or velveteen

Method

See the Pattern on the Pull Out Pattern Sheet.

For the ribbon roses

1 Thread the needle with a thread to match the ribbon. Fold the ribbon at right angles approximately 15 cm (6 in) from the left-hand end. Following the arrow, fold the long part of the ribbon behind the first fold (Fig. 1).

2 Following the arrow in figure 2, fold the ribbon up behind the triangle and hold it firmly in place.

3 Following figure 3, fold the ribbon to the right.

4 Following figure 4, fold the upper end down. Make sure you hold it all firmly together. Continue folding in this way until all the 15 cm (6 in) of the ribbon is folded. Still holding the folded ribbon firmly, gently pull the longer end of the ribbon. Do not pull it too hard or you will lose the centre of your rose and its lovely shape.

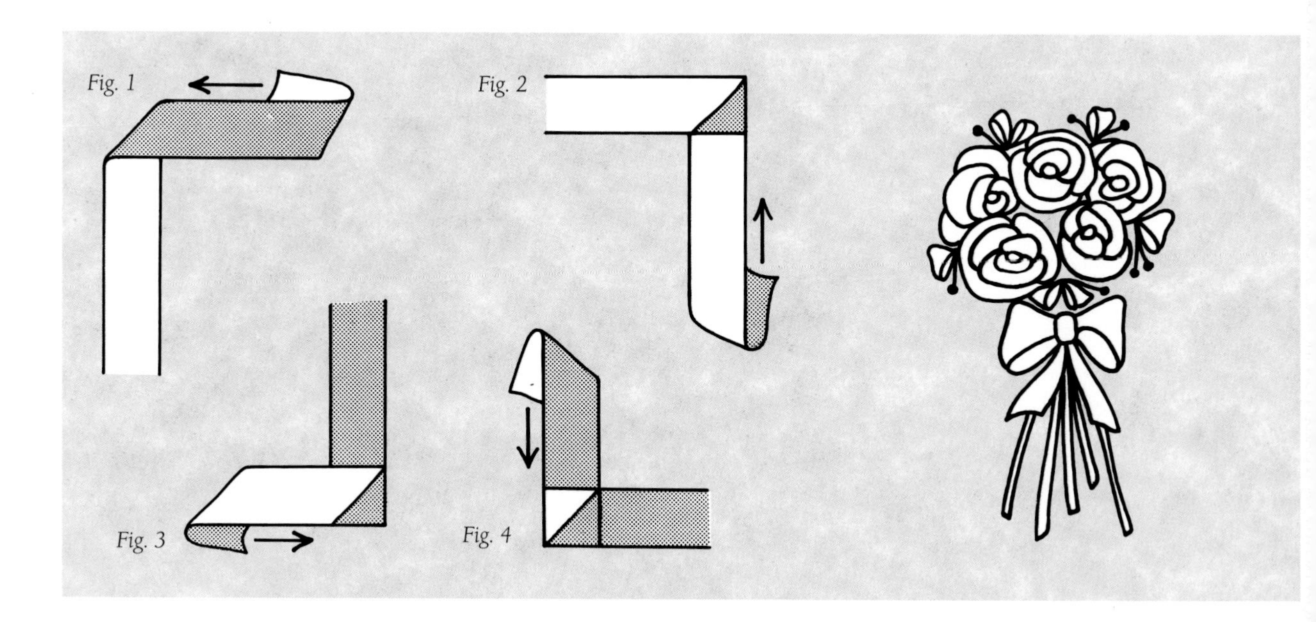

5 Stitch through the centre to the base and around the base to secure the folds of the rose. Cut the rose off from the length of ribbon and set it aside. Make sufficient roses for your posy.

6 Using the pattern, cut one piece of the velvet or velveteen on the bias for the front. Stitch the roses to the velvet in a posy arrangement. Sew three to five beads into the centre of each rose, stitching each bead through the centre of the rose to the back of the velvet to secure.

7 Thread the green ribbon into the tapestry needle and make green ribbon loops around the edges of your posy. Stitch five straight stitch stems.

8 Tie a bow with your chosen ribbon, leaving a long tail. Hand-sew the bow to the base of the roses. Thread each tail of the bow into the tapestry needle and take it to the back of the velvet.

9 Using two strands of the Madeira silk thread and the crewel needle, stitch a few pistol stitch tendrils around the posy.

Assembling

1 Using the pattern, cut one piece of velvet on the straight for the back and two pieces of Pellon.

2 Baste a piece of Pellon to the wrong sides of the front and back of the coathanger. With the right sides together, stitch from the notch at the bottom to the notch at the top. Leaving 1 cm (3/8 in) open at the centre top, stitch to the other bottom notch. Turn the velvet to the right side.

3 Fold the 7 mm (5/16 in) ribbon in half and, with the matching thread, topstitch down both sides. Remove the hook from the coathanger and slip it into the ribbon.

4 Wrap the coathanger in wadding strips, moving from end to end and making sure that each end is well covered. Push a small amount of wadding into each end of the coathanger cover, then pull the cover over the coathanger. Close the opening with a ladder stitch.

5 Starting at the hole at the top, carefully hand-sew the cord around the coathanger seam. Screw in the hook and tie a small bow with the 7 mm (5/16 in) wide ribbon.

Shoe Stuffers

MADE BY FAY KING

Perfect companions for the coathanger, these shoe stuffers can be scented with the addition of some lavender to the filling.

Materials

- **25 cm (10 in) of velvet or cotton velveteen**
- **20 cm (8 in) of lining fabric to match the velvet or velveteen**
- **100 cm (39 in) of 12 mm (1/2 in) wide rayon ribbon in each of two colours**
- **120 cm (48 in) of 2 mm (1/16 in) wide green silk ribbon**
- **25 cm (10 in) of Pellon**
- **rayon ribbon for ties**
- **Mill Hill beads to match the ribbons**
- **threads to match the ribbons**
- **Piecemaker crewel needle, size 9**
- **Piecemaker tapestry needle, size 22**
- **1.25 m (1 1/3 yd) of cord to match the velvet or velveteen**
- **lavender for filling**
- **polyester fibre fill**

Method

See the Pattern on the Pull out Pattern Sheet.

1 Using the pattern, cut two pieces of velvet or velveteen on the bias for the front and two pieces on the straight for the back.

2 Using the pattern again, cut four pieces of Pellon for the 'toe' sections.

3 For each shoe stuffer make and attach three ribbon roses from the rayon ribbon, following the instructions for ribbon roses given on page 18. Complete your arrangement with green silk ribbon loops.

4 Using the pattern lines for the lining, cut four pieces of lining. Stitch one piece at the straight end of each velvet or velveteen piece with the right sides facing and using a 6 mm (1/4 in) seam allowance.

5 Lay one piece of Pellon on the wrong side of each velvet piece and baste them together. With right sides together, stitch each pair together from the edge of the lining around the 'toe' to the other edge of the lining. Turn the shoe stuffer to the right side. Fold the lining into the centre and secure the lining on each side seam to hold it in place.

6 Hand-sew the cord over the seam with small stitches, taking it over the lined edge into the shoe stuffer.

7 Fill the toe firmly with the polyester fibre fill, adding approximately 2.5 cm (1 in) of lavender in the middle. Fill up to the dotted line.

8 Run a gathering thread around at the dotted line. Pull the thread up firmly to gather and close the shoe stuffer. Finish with a beautiful bow.

Baby's Silk Quilt

MADE BY PAT FLYNN KYSER

This feather-light silk quilt is a delight for a special baby. Embroider a garland of your favourite flowers in silk ribbons and a special motif in the centre, if you wish.

Materials

- **107 cm (42 in) square of silk batiste in the colour of your choice for the top**
- **107 cm (42 in) square of white Swiss cotton batiste for the lining**
- **107 cm (42 in) square of fine lightweight polyester wadding**
- **107 cm (42 in) square of white Swiss cotton batiste for the backing**
- **30 cm (12 in) strip cut across the width of the white Swiss batiste for binding**
- **2 mm and 4 mm (1/16 in and 3/16 in) wide silk ribbons in your chosen colours for the flower embroidery**
- **DMC stranded cotton for embroidering the stems and leaves and the central motif**
- **Piecemaker tapestry needle**
- **Piecemaker embroidery needle, size 9**
- **Piecemaker quilting needle, size 9**
- **fine cotton quilting thread**
- **66 cm (26 in) embroidery hoop**
- **water-soluble marker pen**
- **store-bought quilting templates for the corners**

Method

Preparation

1 Fold the coloured silk batiste into halves, then into quarters, then into eighths and lightly finger-crease the folds to find the centre. Using the water-soluble pen, draw an arc across each eighth 30.5 cm (12 in) from the centre and again 15.25 cm (6 in) from the centre to form two scalloped circles 15.25 cm (6 in) apart.

2 Using the water-soluble pen and the embroidery hoop, mark a circle 66 cm (26 in) in diameter between the two scalloped circles. Baste in this circle. If you wish to embroider a motif in the centre, trace it with the water-soluble pen.

3 Fold the cotton batiste into halves, then into quarters and lightly mark the folds. Baste this piece to the back of the silk piece along the fold lines. Baste diagonally from corner to corner and around the edges. Baste around the circle on the silk batiste, catching the cotton batiste with each stitch. Working your embroidery through the two layers joined in this way will anchor the embroidery and prevent it from pulling through the delicate silk top.

Embroidery

1 Secure the centre of the piece in the embroidery hoop and embroider your central design with DMC stranded threads. Make sure each stitch goes right through both pieces of fabric and ensure that thread ends are well hidden behind the cotton batiste.

2 Using the tapestry needle and your choice of silk ribbons, embroider a wreath of flowers, including wisteria, roses, rose buds, forget-me-nots and daisies, along the basted circle. Use the Embroidery Guide on page 32 to help you choose and work the flowers. Work randomly, going around the circle first with one kind of flower, then going back around the circle and filling in with another flower and so on. Do not make the flowers perfectly spaced or identical. You should try to create a spontaneous light and airy appearance.

3 Keep working around the wreath in this manner until it is as full as you want it to be. Go back and work in the stems and some leaves in both the DMC stranded thread and silk ribbon. Again, try to avoid symmetry.

Quilting

1 Place the backing face down with the wadding on top and the embroidered top on top of that, face up. Baste through all the layers, horizontally, vertically, diagonally and around the edges.

BABY'S TEETHING RING AND WHISTLE, MOSMAN ANTIQUE CENTRE, MOSMAN, NSW

2 Place the quilt top in the 66 cm (26 in) hoop. Using the quilting thread and quilting needle, quilt double lines 6 mm (1/4 in) apart, inside the inner scallop. Quilt a double diagonal grid from the embroidered centre to the inner scalloped circle. Place these grid lines 12 mm (1/2 in) apart. To create a true lattice-like appearance, weave these quilted lines over at one intersection and under at the next.

3 With single rows of stitches, firmly quilt the large scalloped ring outside the floral wreath.

4 Use a store-bought template, such as a feathered wreath or a heart, for the corner quilting patterns. Using the water-soluble pen, mark one in each corner.

5 Draw a 12 mm (1/2 in) diagonal grid from corner to corner of the quilt, ending at the outer scalloped circle and covering the areas not already quilted. Quilt along these lines, through all thicknesses. Quilt the designs in the corners as you come to them.

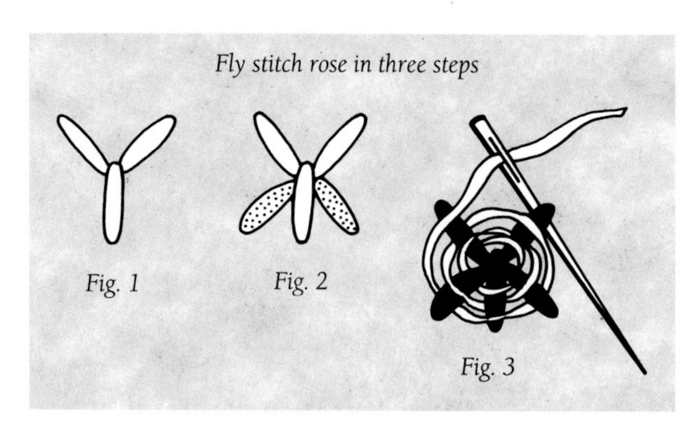

To complete

1 Cut the fabric for the binding into four 7.5 cm (3 in) strips. Fold them over double with the wrong sides together. Pin the binding to the sides of the quilt on the right side, with the raw edges matching. Stitch 12 mm (1/2 in) from the edge. Repeat for the top and bottom of the quilt. Turn the folded edge of the binding to the wrong side of the quilt and slipstitch it into place.

2 Embroider your name, the date, the baby's name and birth date on the back of the quilt.

3 Soak the quilt in clean cold water just long enough to remove all traces of the marker pen. Dry flat.

Doll's Dress

MADE BY ANNE'S GLORY BOX

Smocking is the ideal finish for this smart Victorian-style dress. Pick out the colours from the Liberty cotton print for the embroidery.

To fit: a 76 cm (30 in) doll

Materials

- **1.6 m (1 3/4 yd) of Liberty fabric**
- **4 m (4 1/2 yd) of 9 cm (3 1/2 in) wide Swiss embroidery**
- **60 cm (24 in) of 4 cm (1 1/2 in) wide Swiss embroidery**
- **DMC stranded thread: Burgundy, Green, Ecru**
- **1.5 m (1 2/3 yd) of 3.5 cm (1 3/8 in) wide cream satin ribbon**
- **1 m (1 1/8 yd) of 6 mm (1/4 in) wide cream satin ribbon**
- **1 m (1 1/8 yd) of 6 mm (1/4 in) wide entredeux**
- **Piecemaker crewel needle, size 8**
- **press studs**
- **smocking pleater (optional)**

Method

See the Pattern and the Smocking Plate on the Pull Out Pattern Sheet.

For the smocking

1 Cut one piece of fabric for the front, 35 cm x 90 cm (13 3/4 in x 35 1/2 in) and two pieces for the backs, each 35 cm x 45 cm (13 3/4 in x 17 3/4 in).

2 At the top edge of the front, draw up seven half-space rows with the smocking pleater, unless you prefer to use the smocking service provided by your local haberdashery store.

3 Undo the pleating for 1.5 cm (5/8 in) from each edge and tie the threads off evenly in pairs.

4 Complete the smocking as shown on the smocking plate, then block the smocking to fit the front bodice.

For the bodice and sleeves

1 Join the front and back yokes at the shoulders, using a 6 mm (1/4 in) seam.

2 Cut a small piece of fabric, 5 cm x 35 cm (2 in x 13 3/4 in), on the bias. Press the piece over double with the wrong sides together.

3 Gather the narrow Swiss embroidery to fit the neck edge. Pin the gathered Swiss embroidery around the neck edge, both with right sides up. Adjust the gathering to ensure that it is even.

4 Pin the bias strip around the neck edge, over the Swiss embroidery, with all the raw edges even. Stitch. Turn the folded edge to the wrong side and slipstitch it into place, neatening the ends as you go.

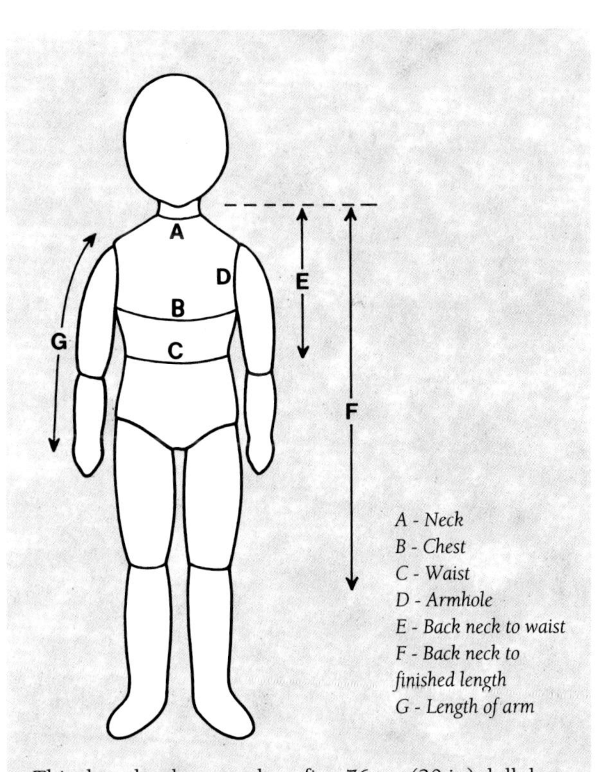

This dress has been made to fit a 76 cm (30 in) doll, but it is quite simple to adjust the pattern to suit a different-sized doll. Measure all the areas indicated in the diagram, then adjust the pattern accordingly. For awkward or very small measurements, use cotton tape or string to measure your doll, then check the length on a tape measure.

5 Sew entredeux around the sleeve ends. Gather the wide Swiss embroidery slightly and attach it to the entredeux.

6 Gather the sleeve heads as marked. Insert the sleeves into the armholes, pulling up the gathering to fit.

For the skirt

1 Gather the skirt backs to fit the yokes, then attach them, using 6 mm (1/4 in) seams.

2 Pin and baste the smocked front skirt to the front yoke, making sure the stitching is straight above the even smocking pleats.

3 Stitch the skirt side seams and the underarm seams in one go.

4 At the bottom edge of the skirt, stitch two pintucks, 6.5 cm (2 1/2 in) and 4.5 cm (1 3/4 in) from the edge.

5 Cut three pieces of fabric, each 15 cm x 90 cm (5 7/8 in x 35 1/2 in), for the frill. Join them to make one long strip. Neaten the two raw ends. Make a 6 mm (1/4 in) hem on one long edge. On the other long edge, baste a length of the wide Swiss embroidery with both the fabric and the Swiss embroidery facing upwards. Gather them as one. Pin the ruffle to the skirt, adjusting the gathering to fit. Stitch, then neaten the seam.

6 Neaten the raw centre back edges and press them to the wrong side. Sew press studs down the back edge, fixing the hem at the same time. Neatly attach the wider ribbon for ties at the edges of the smocking. Run the narrower cream satin ribbon through the entredeux to gather up the sleeve ends.

Gloria's tips
for Successful Smocking

Smocking pleaters make light work of pulling up the pleats for smocking. An even easier way to get the job done is to use the pleating service provided by stores.

When putting the fabric through a smocking pleater, the right side of the fabric should face the floor of the pleater.

Before using your smocking pleater, run a piece of waxed lunchwrap through it. This will lubricate the needles and allow the fabric to pass through more easily. Only use the number of needles you actually need.

When you have cut the stranded thread, separate the six strands and put them back together in two groups of three strands. Knot them together at the cut end. This process will eliminate tangling and twisting of the thread.

It is important to straighten the edges of the fabric you are going to smock by pulling threads. Fabrics cut on the grain will pleat more easily than those cut against the grain.

Usually, the smocked piece is tied off 2.5–4 cm (1–1 1/2 in) smaller than the finished piece will be, otherwise the smocking will need to be stretched too much and may cause ripples when it is attached. Remember to use a reef knot when you tie off your smocking.

Garden Lambs Blanket

EMBROIDERED BY GLORIA MCKINNON

Baby lambs and spring flowers adorn this charming blanket, which would be a perfect project for a novice embroiderer.

Materials

- **80 cm x 115 cm (31½ in x 45 in) of blanket wool**
- **assortment of Piecemaker tapestry needles, sizes 20 and 22**
- **DMC tapestry wool: White, Yellow, Pale Pink, Pale Blue, Blue, Green, Black**
- **Appleton's Crewel Wool: Pale Pink, Pale Blue, Lemon**
- **2.4 m (2⅔ yd) of Liberty fabric OR 140 cm (55 in) of another 115 cm (45 in) wide fabric for the backing**
- **15 cm (6 in) of fabric for piping**
- **4 m (4½ yd) of piping cord**

Method

See the Embroidery Guide and Key on the Pull Out Pattern Sheet.

1 Mark a line 45 cm (17⅔ in) from the top edge of the blanket with a row of stitches. This will be your placement guide for the top row of lambs. The second group of lambs is embroidered approximately 5 cm (2 in) below the first group.

2 Embroider the lambs and flowers, following the embroidery guide and key and figures 1 to 3.

For the piping

1 Cut five strips, each 2.5 cm (1 in) wide, across the width of the piping fabric. Cut off the selvages, then join the strips to make one long strip.

2 Fold the fabric over double, with the wrong sides together and the piping cord sandwiched in between.

3 Using the zipper foot on your sewing machine, stitch along the length of the strip, stitching as close as possible to the piping cord.

Assembling

1 Cut the backing fabric into two 1.2 m (1⅓ yd) lengths. Cut off the selvages, then rejoin the pieces down the 1.2 m (1⅓ yd) sides to achieve the required width. Press the seam open.

2 Lay the backing face down on a table. Lay the embroidered blanket on the backing, face upwards. Baste from the centre outwards to the edges and the corners to hold the whole arrangement together securely as you work.

3 Trim the backing so that it is 10 cm (4 in) bigger than the embroidered blanket all around.

4 Pin the piping to the embroidered blanket, 5 cm (2 in) from the edge. To help ease the piping around the corners, clip the seam allowance of the piping at least three times at each corner.

5 Trim the ends of the piping so that one end is 2.5 cm (1 in) longer than the other. Undo the stitching for 2.5 cm (1 in) on the longer end, pull back the fabric and cut off 2.5 cm (1 in) of the cord so that the two ends of the cord meet exactly. Fold under 1.25 cm (½ in) on the end of the fabric and place the other (shorter) end of the piping inside. Stitch the piping in place all around.

6 Fold the edge of the backing to meet the blanket, then fold it again to meet the piping. Pin the fabric in place. Carefully fold the corners into mitres, then slipstitch the backing into place, stitching through the piping and the blanket but not through the backing fabric. Stitch the mitres into place. Make sure that the machine-stitching on the piping is covered by the backing.

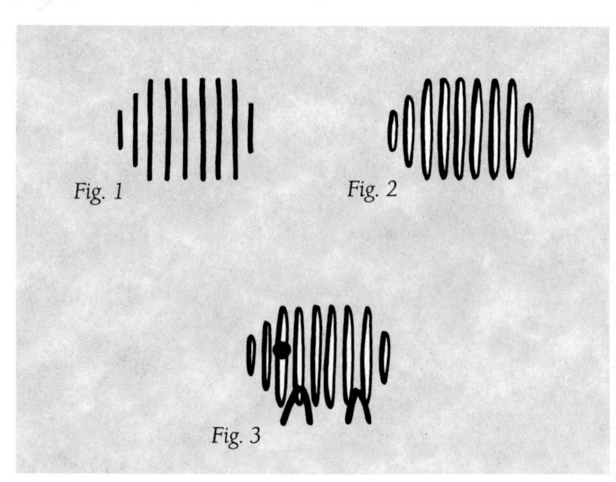

Découpage Brooches

MADE BY KARA KING

What could be more romantic than a brooch featuring roses or a Victorian beauty, made using a technique popular in that era.

Choosing the right image is crucial for making this brooch. Consider carefully the size or the picture and whether you wish to use one large picture or several small ones. Enthusiastic découpeurs are always on the lookout for interesting pictures they can store away for just the right project.

Materials

- **wooden brooch (oval or round)**
- **brooch back**
- **suitable images**
- **FolkArt Acrylic BaseCoat**
- **gold paint**
- **Liquitex Sealer**
- **craft glue**
- **rubber roller**
- **fine-pointed sharp curved scissors**
- **Clag paste**
- **PVA adhesive**
- **clear varnish**
- **paintbrushes**
- **brushes for sealer and glue**
- **sable brush for varnish**
- **wet and dry sandpaper, 600 grade**
- **tack cloth**

Method

1 Paint the front and back of the brooch with two coats of acrylic paint, allowing the paint to dry thoroughly between coats.

2 Mix three parts of Clag to one part of PVA adhesive, making sure the mixture is quite smooth with no lumps. Spread some of the glue mixture on the brooch, then place the image or images on the glued surface. Add a little more glue to the face of the image, spreading it with your fingers to test for lumps. Using the rubber roller, gently roll from the centre out to the edges. Remove any excess glue from the roller.

3 Using your finger, rub a little gold paint around the edge of the brooch.

4 When the glue and the paint are quite dry, coat the face of the brooch with two coats of Liquitex Sealer.

5 Using the sable brush, apply at least twelve coats of varnish, each one in the opposite direction to the last, and allowing twelve hours between the coats. It is also a good idea to wipe the brooch with a tack cloth between coats to remove all traces of dust.

6 Sand the brooch lightly with the wet and dry sandpaper to remove any bumps and ridges. Wipe with the tack cloth, then apply two coats of varnish in as dust-free an environment as you can manage. Finally, glue on the brooch back with the craft glue.

Silk Ribbon Embroidery

Iris

Make these using 7 mm (5/16 in) silk ribbon.

Stitch the leaves and stems in straight stitches. Work an open fly stitch, then work a straight stitch through the securing loop at the bottom, allowing it to curve gently.

Violet

Work the violet petals in straight stitches using 4 mm (3/16 in) violet silk ribbon. Work a French knot in the centre using a gold thread.

Violet leaves are worked in blanket stitch, using 4 mm (3/16 in) rich green silk ribbon.

Leaves

Groups of leaves are worked in the same way as the wheat, using 4 mm (3/16 in) green ribbon. Small leaves are worked with straight stitches, using 4 mm (3/16 in) silk ribbon.

Fuschia

Fuschias are made in 7 mm (5/16 in) silk ribbon in two shades of pink.

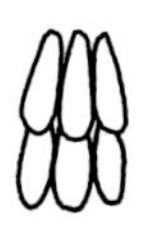

For the base, using the paler pink and beginning with the bottom layer, work two straight stitches side by side with a third straight stitch worked loosely across the bottom of the first two.

Work a floppy open fly stitch at the top in the darker pink.

Form the stamens in pistol stitch (a straight stitch anchored at one end with a French knot) in the darker pink.

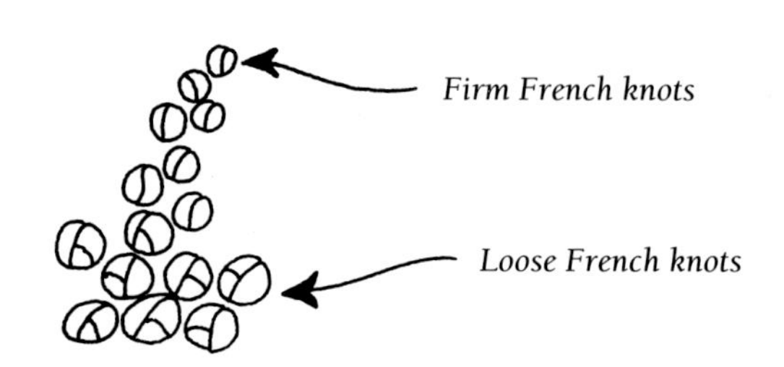

Grape hyacinth

Using 2 mm (1/16 in) silk ribbon, work graded French knots from loose at the bottom to very tight at the top.

Silk rose

Tiny silk roses are worked in three shades of the same colour: a light, medium and dark.

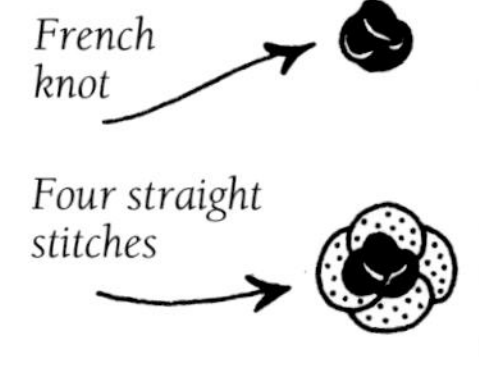

Six or seven straight stitches

Begin with a French knot centre in the darkest shade. Work four straight stitches around the centre in the medium shade, then work six or seven straight stitches around the outside in the lightest shade.

For the rosebud, work a French knot in the centre in the darkest shade, then work two straight stitches on either side of the French knot in the medium shade.

Ribbon stitch

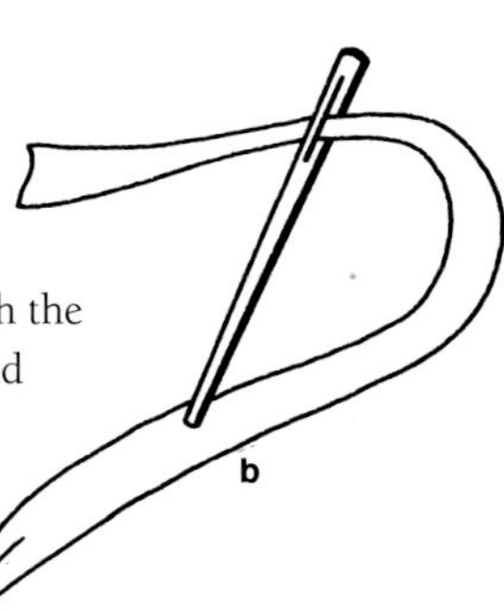

Bring the needle through from the back of the work at **a**. Take the needle through to the back by passing it through the ribbon at **b**. Don't pull the thread through too tightly or you will lose the little loop at the top.

Lazy daisy stitch

Lazy daisy stitch is the basic stitch for many embroidered flowers. Take care when you are working this stitch not to pull the ribbon too tightly or you will lose the softness of the ribbon.

For lazy daisy stitch, bring the needle through from the back at the centre point of the flower. Take the needle back through to the back of the work at a point very close to where it emerged.

Secure the loop you have just made with a tiny stitch across the loop, then bring the needle back to the centre ready to begin the next petal.

French knot

French knots are ideal for flower centres. Begin by bringing the needle up through the fabric where you wish the knot to sit. Wind the ribbon around the needle twice. Gently pulling the thread tight, reinsert the needle near the point of exit and pull it through, bringing the needle out at the point you wish to make the next stitch.

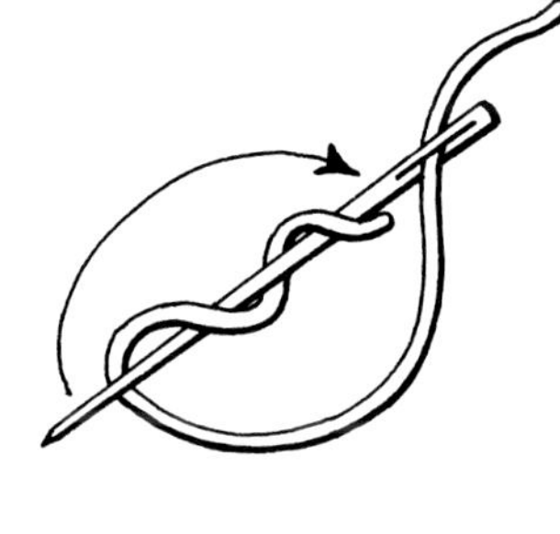

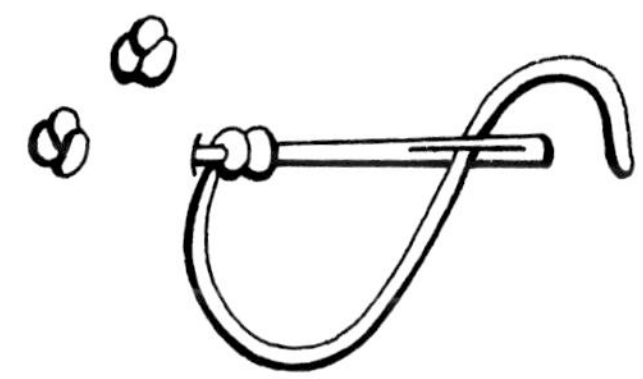

Fly stitch rose

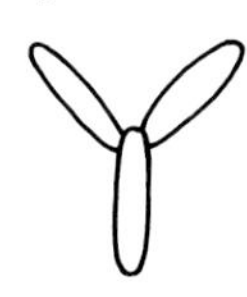

Using 4 mm ribbon and size 22 tapestry needle, make one open fly stitch, approximately this size.

Then add two straight stitches to make five arms or spokes.

Do not end off – bring needle up close to the centre, but do not pierce the existing ribbon; and weave the ribbon around these five arms (under, over, under, etc.) Travelling right around ten to twelve times. Allow the ribbon to twist to form more realistic petals. If desired, you can change colour after weaving three or four times in the first colour, using a lighter shade on the last seven or eight rounds .

Wisteria

Using 4 mm (3/16 in) lilac silk ribbon and beginning at the top, make a group of colonial knots.

Add a few French knots towards the bottom.

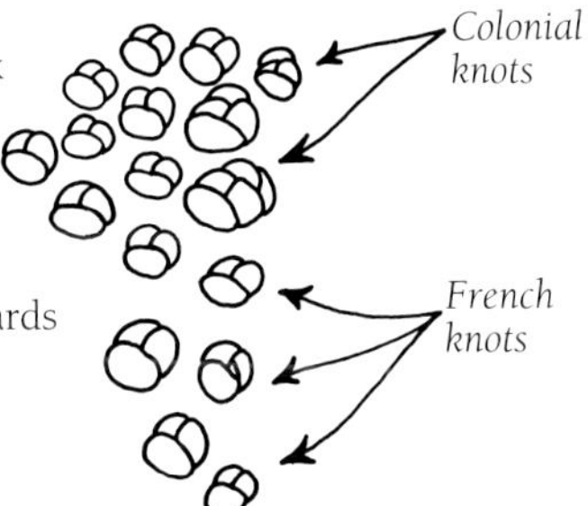

Lace Roses

MADE BY FAY KING

Ecru lace roses on a navy velvet background make this elegant piece that is really quite simple to create.

Materials

- **4.6 m (5 yd) of 10 cm (4 in) wide single-edge ecru Swiss needlerun lace**
- **1.5 m (1 2/3 yd) of 12 mm (1/2 in) wide rayon ribbon, green**
- **50 cm (20 in) of cotton velveteen, navy**
- **50 cm (20 in) of Pellon**
- **one spool of cream quilting thread**
- **picture frame**
- **1.5 m (1 2/3 yd) of 4 cm (1 1/2 in) wide ribbon**

Method

For the roses

1 Cut five pieces of lace, each 75 cm (30 in) long. Fold over the embroidered edge for approximately 2 cm (3/4 in) at one end. Beginning at this end, roll the lace tightly four times for the centre of the rose. Using the quilting thread, stitch through the lace at the bottom to hold the centre securely.

2 Continue folding and rolling the lace around the centre, allowing the turns to become looser as you approach the outside of the rose. Stitch to secure as before.

3 Wrap quilting thread tightly around the base of the rose six or eight times, then trim any excess lace at the base. With your fingers, fold and arrange the top edge of the lace to resemble a rose.

For the buds

1 Cut three pieces of lace, each 25 cm (10 in) long. Roll the lace tightly for eight turns as for the centre of the rose, then fold the embroidered edge over and roll more loosely for the remainder of the length.

2 Stitch through the base with the quilting thread, then wind the thread around the base as before.

For the leaves

1 For each bud, cut two pieces of green ribbon, each 10 cm (4 in) long. Fold the ribbon as shown in figure 1.

2 Stitch across the base of the leaf, then pull up the stitching to gather the leaf. Stitch the leaves to the base of the buds.

Assembling

1 Baste the Pellon to the back of the velveteen. Arrange the five roses and three buds into a posy. Stitch each flower and bud securely to the velveteen, taking care that the velveteen does not pucker.

2 Tie a beautiful bow and attach it at the bottom of the posy with a few stitches.

3 Have your picture framed with a fabulous gilt frame which allows some depth.

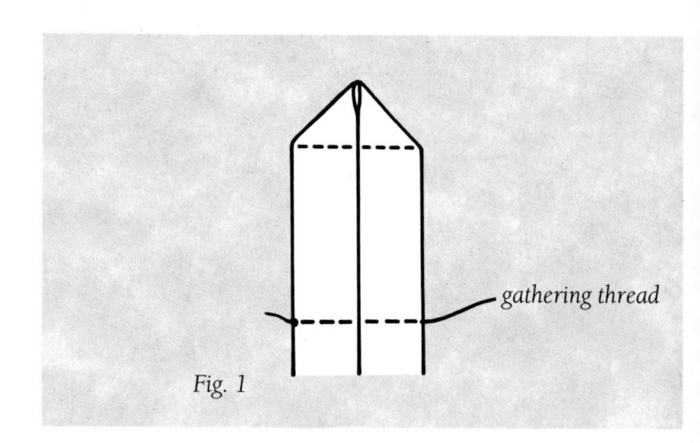

Fig. 1

Rose Shoes and Purse

MADE BY MARGARET B. WOLFE

This delightful set of evening shoes and matching bag is quite simple to make when you have mastered the basic rose.

All the roses are made in exactly the same way. The apparent variety is provided by the use of ribbons of different textures, widths and colours.

Materials

- **pump-style fabric-covered shoes**
- **purse, either purchased or handmade**
- **variety of ribbons including silk, velvet, metallic and French wired ribbon**
- **E6000 glue**
- **sewing needle**
- **sewing thread to match the ribbons**
- **chenille needle or tapestry needle**
- **hat pin or toothpick**
- **fine wire or Bouillion**
- **corrugated cardboard or styrofoam**
- **plastic wrap**
- **crinoline**

Method

For the rosebuds

1 For each rosebud, you will need seven times the width of the ribbon you are using. Beginning close to one end of the ribbon, fold down the end diagonally (Fig. 1).

2 Fold the width of the ribbon in half again, folding diagonally (Fig. 2). Fold again in the same manner (Fig. 3).

3 Insert a hat pin or a toothpick into the folds and roll the ribbon up around the pin or toothpick to form the centre of the rosebud (Fig. 4). Remove the pin, but keep a firm hold with your thumb and index finger to prevent it unrolling again.

4 Fold the loose part of the ribbon away from you, again folding on the diagonal. Still holding the base with your thumb and index finger, roll in the direction indicated by the arrow (Fig. 5). In order to roll the base of the rosebud along the inner edge of the ribbon, you will automatically force the folded edge of the ribbon to remain at the top of the rosebud and flare out just slightly. When you have 'used up' the folded edge, fold the ribbon away from you again, just as you did the first time. Continue to fold and roll in this way until you have used all the ribbon, leaving a tail approximately 2.5 cm (1 in) long.

5 Sew a row of gathering stitches across the tail end of the ribbon (Fig. 6). Remove the needle but do not cut the thread. Draw up the gathering then secure the end to the base of the rosebud with a few stitches. Wrap the thread several times around the base of the rosebud, then secure it with a knot (Fig. 7).

For the full bloom

1 This rose is best worked with wired ribbon. You will need a length that is twelve to fourteen times the width of the ribbon. Every fold you make will stay in place if you crimp the wire slightly. Begin by following steps 1 to 5 for the rosebud to make a centre for the rose. Secure the base of the centre with a few stitches, then cut the thread.

2 Carefully remove the wire from the bottom edge of the remaining ribbon. Gather the bottom edge (Fig. 8). Loosely wrap the gathering around the base. Pinch in the loose end and secure it in place with some wire or with a few stitches.

3 Flatten the rose with your hand or, very gently, with a steam iron. Arrange the 'petals' attractively, crimping and pinching the wired edge to create a pleasing shape.

For the leaf

1 For this leaf, use a length of wired ribbon, seven to ten times the width of the ribbon. Carefully pull out 12 mm ($^1/_2$ in) of the wire from the same side of both cut ends of the ribbon. Gripping these ends of wire between your thumb and index finger, continue working the ribbon onto the wire until it is fully gathered (Fig. 9).

2 Pinch the cut ends together and wind the wire around to form the stem (Fig. 10).

3 To close the centre 'seam' of the leaf, apply a small amount of E6000 and press the edges together for a few seconds.

For the loop rosette

1 Use 30.5-35.5 cm (12-14 in) of 3 mm (1/8 in) metallic or silk ribbon. Using matching thread and a needle, take small stitches along the ribbon at approximately 2.5-4 cm (1-1 1/2 in) intervals, beginning and ending approximately 2.5 cm (1 in) from the end of the ribbon (Fig. 11).

2 Pull up the thread to form the rosette. Secure the thread with a lock stitch (Fig. 12).

For the vines

Make shiny vines by coiling fine wire tightly onto a toothpick or chenille or tapestry needle. Remove the toothpick or needle, then pull the coil slightly to extend the vine. There is available a very tightly coiled super-fine wire material, called Bouillion, which is ideal. This delightful stuff comes in copper, silver and gold.

For the flat bud or leaf

1 Using a length of ribbon four times the width of the ribbon, fold one end down as shown in figure 13.

2 Cross-fold the ribbon and sew a gathering thread across (Fig. 14). Pull up the thread tightly, then wrap the thread around the ends of the ribbon to form a stem (Fig. 15).

Assembling

1 Cover a 25 cm (10 in) square of corrugated cardboard or styrofoam with plastic wrap. This will be your work surface.

2 Arrange your composition of roses, leaves, rosettes and vines on a piece of crinoline that is approximately the size of the shoe front or the purse flap. Remember to use black crinoline for dark colours and white for pastels. Any excess crinoline can be cut away from the back when the whole arrangement is assembled. Place the piece of crinoline on the work surface. Begin by placing the leaves and flat buds in position. Next, place your focal flower, usually the largest rose. Add in the smaller roses, rosebuds, leaves, loop rosettes and vines. These filler pieces can be tucked into empty spaces or be peeping out from behind a larger flower.

3 When you are pleased with your arrangement, glue it into place on the crinoline. Trim the crinoline from the back, then glue the crimoline into place on the shoes and the purse.

To learn know more about this charming craft, read *Small Treasures in Victorian Ribbonwork* by Margaret B. Wolfe.

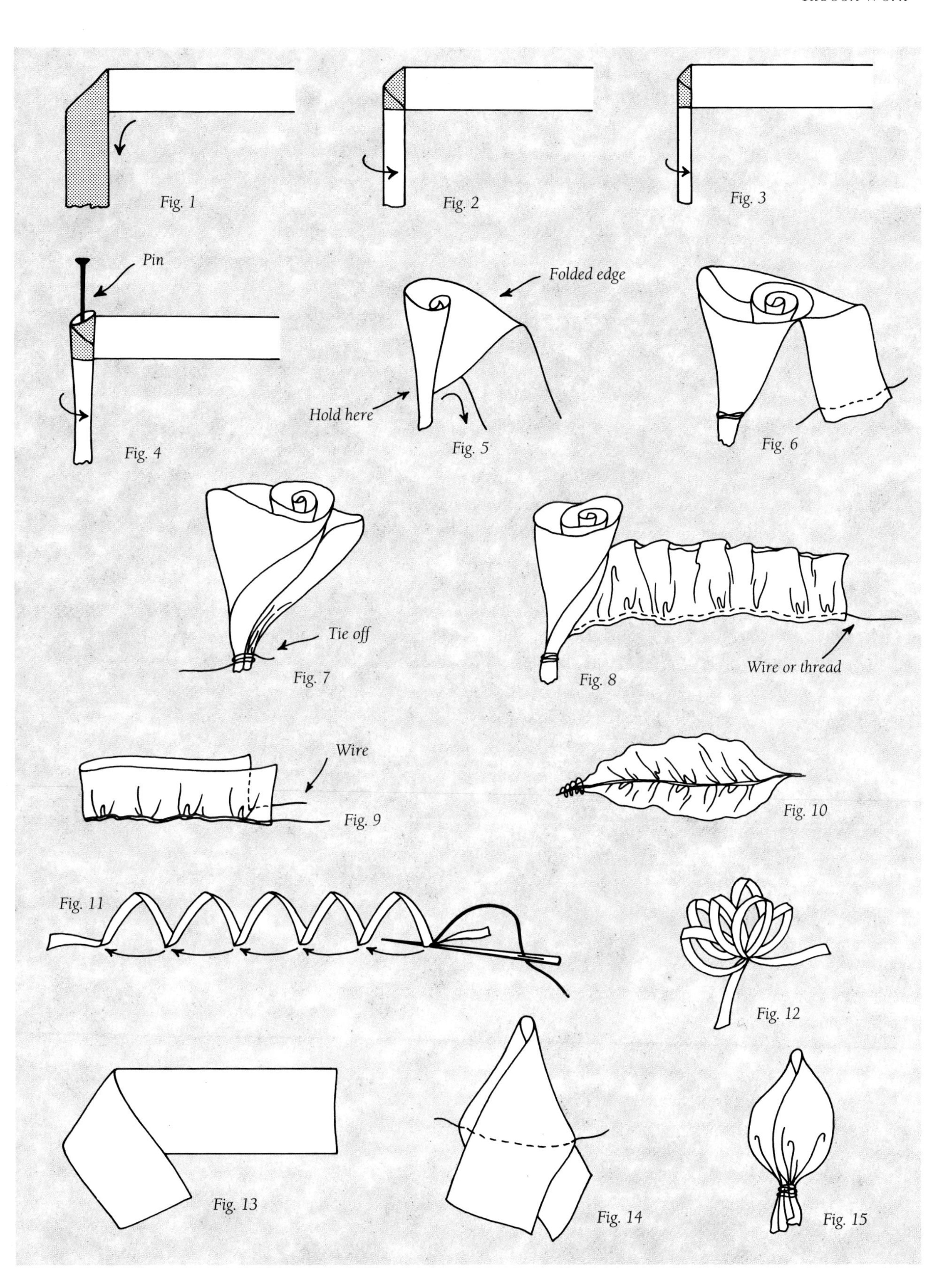
Fig. 1
Fig. 2
Fig. 3
Pin
Fig. 4
Folded edge
Hold here
Fig. 5
Fig. 6
Tie off
Fig. 7
Fig. 8
Wire or thread
Wire
Fig. 9
Fig. 10
Fig. 11
Fig. 12
Fig. 13
Fig. 14
Fig. 15

Crazy Quilt

This magnificent old quilt is a perfect example of a style of quilt which was most popular in the last quarter of the nineteenth century.

Such quilts were made using foundation pieces of fabric which were the size of the finished block. This piece was covered, in an apparently haphazard way, with fabrics of every kind – especially silks and satins – and then heavily embellished with embroidery, silks and laces. Fabrics from men's ties, cravats and waistcoats were frequently used, because they had a special richness of colour that added great depth to the work.

In the Victorian era, middle class parlours were full of clutter, and the crazy patchwork style was seen to reflect this mood both in its irregularity and its opulence.

To make your own crazy patchwork quilt, gather up a collection of suitable fabrics, such as silks, satins, velvets, taffetas, moirés, jewel-coloured prints, laces, tulles . . . and as many unwanted men's ties as you can muster. The patchwork technique is exactly the same as for the purse on page 42, but clearly the scale is larger. Use as many embroidery stitches as you can; the greater variety adds to the random appearance. There are some additional embroidery stitches provided for you to use on page 44. Traditionally, the embroidery included animal and bird designs, flowers and leaves, and almost always a spider web complete with spider.

When your quilt top is assembled, complete it as you would any other quilt, but take great care with any pressing you do.

Crazy Quilt Purse

STITCHED BY JUDITH MONTANO

This lovely patchwork purse has been richly embellished with embroidery, sequins, special buttons and charms. Judith's work and her use of colour are quite exceptional. Adding your own embellishments to the basic design will make it unique to you.

Finished size (closed): 14 cm x 18 cm ($5^1/2$ in x 7 in)

Materials

- **scraps of silk, satin and cotton fabrics**
- **30 cm (12 in) of velvet, ultrasuede or heavy moiré or other suitable fabric**
- **18 cm x 30 cm (7 in x 12 in) of homespun**
- **18 cm x 30 cm (7 in x 12 in) of iron-on interfacing**
- **30 cm (12 in) Pellon**
- **silk buttonhole twist or embroidery floss in an assortment of colours**
- **metallic threads**
- **beads, buttons, brass charms**
- **3 m ($3^1/4$ yd) each of cord in four or five assorted colours and thicknesses**
- **three large buttons**
- **water-soluble marker pen**
- **tacky glue**

Method

See the Pattern on the Pull Out Pattern Sheet.

1 Cut out the pattern pieces from the homespun, interfacing and velvet, ultrasuede or moiré as instructed on the pattern.

Note: When cutting pattern piece A from the homespun, allow an additional 12 mm ($^1/2$ in) all around. This piece will be trimmed after all the embellishments are added.

2 Begin creating the patchwork from the centre of the piece. From a dark solid fabric, cut a five-sided shape. Pin it to the approximate centre of the homespun piece A.

3 From another fabric, cut a rectangle that will cover one edge of the centre piece. Lay this piece on the centre piece with the right sides together and stitch in a 6 mm ($^1/4$ in) seam. Trim the seam allowance back to 3 mm ($^1/8$ in). Press the rectangle back.

4 Working clockwise around the centre piece, continue adding rectangles until each side of the centre piece has been stitched (Fig 1). Trim the free edges to create new angles and five new sides (Fig. 2). Continue to add pieces, keeping a balance of colour, texture, prints and plains.

5 When the homespun is covered, place pattern piece A over it and mark the shape with the water-soluble pen.

6 Stitch assorted laces and ribbons onto the patchwork piece. Cover all the seam lines with embroidery stitches, following the stitch guide on page 44, then sew on the beads, buttons and charms.

Assembling

1 Fuse the interfacing to the wrong side of the patchwork piece, the wrong side of the velvet, ultrasuede or moiré piece A and the wrong side of the velvet piece B.

2 Lay the velvet piece A on the table, facing upwards. Place the quilted piece on top, face down, then the Pellon. Pin the layers together. Stitch around the edge in a 1 cm ($^3/8$ in) seam, leaving a 5 cm (2 in) opening on one side. Trim the seam allowance, then turn the piece through to the right side. Slipstitch the opening closed. Press.

3 Place the two velvet pieces B together with the right sides facing and a piece of Pellon on top. Pin, stitch, turn and press as for the A piece.

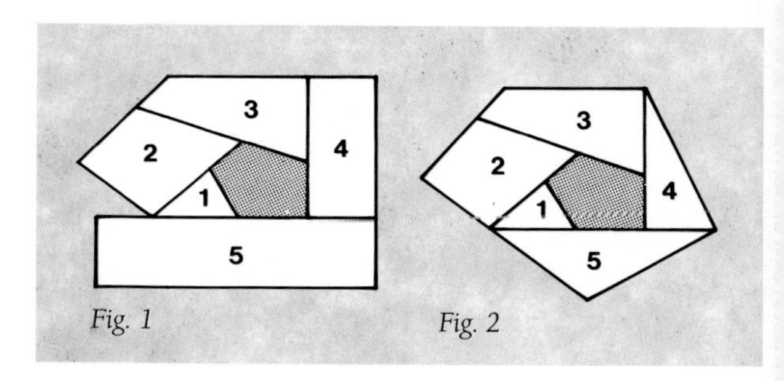

Fig. 1 *Fig. 2*

4 Whipstitch the front and back together as shown on the pattern.

5 Whipstitch a length of cord along the edge of the flap, making a loop in the centre for the closure.

6 Braid the rest of the cords together to make a 140 cm (55 in) length. Tie the ends together, leaving approximately 5–8 cm (2–3 in) below the knot for a tassel.

7 Lay a narrow bead of glue around the edge of the purse. Pin the cord over the glued edge with the tassel at the bottom. Allow the glue to dry, then whipstitch the cord into place.

8 Sew one button at each side of the top and one button to close the purse.

Stitch Guide

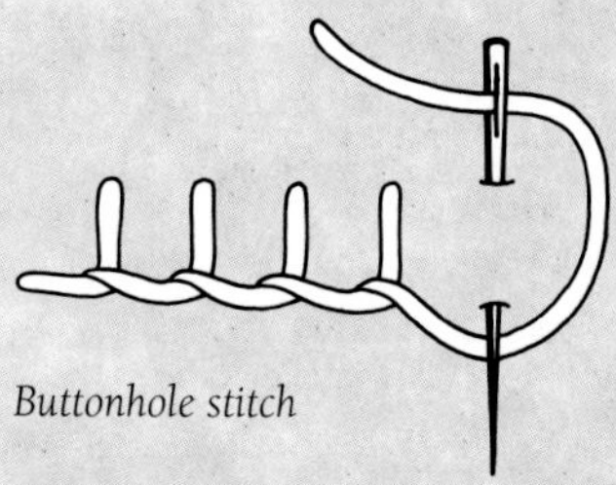

Buttonhole stitch

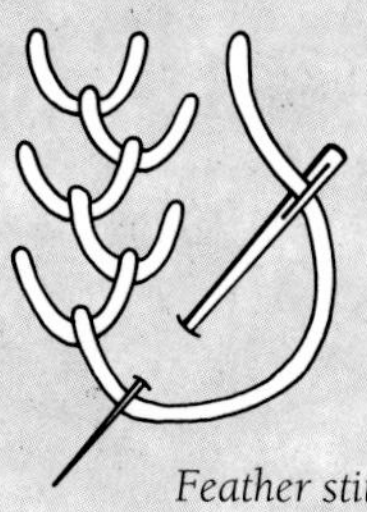

Feather stitch

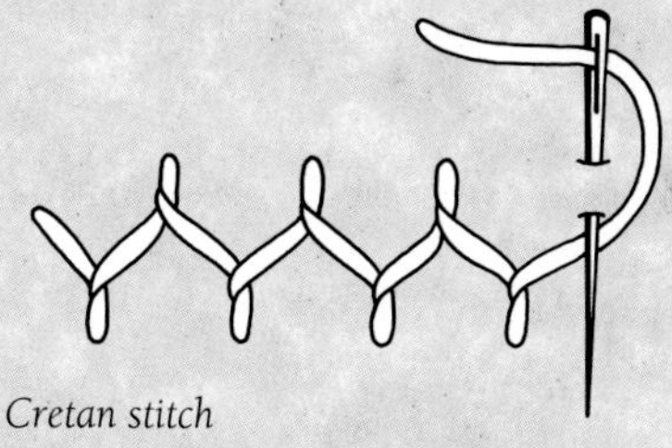

Cretan stitch

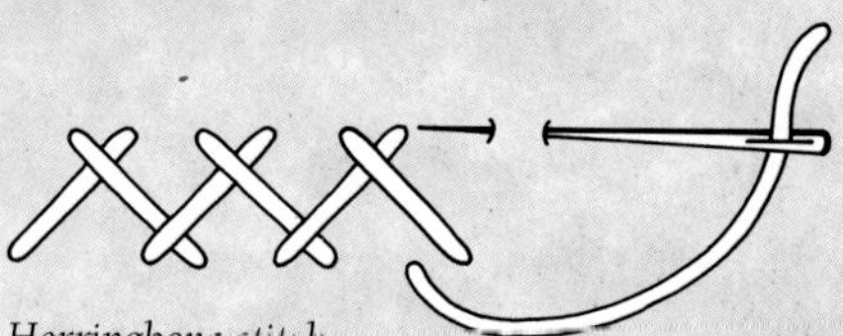

Herringbone stitch

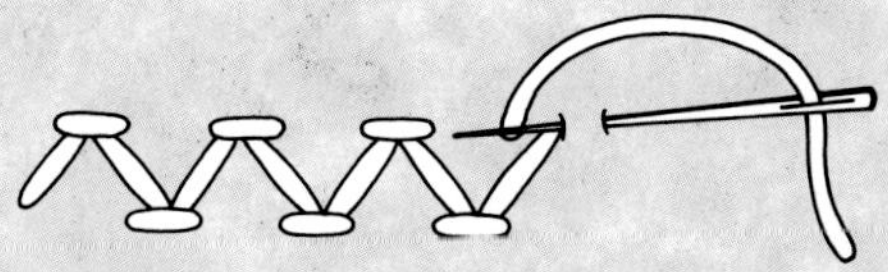

Chevron stitch

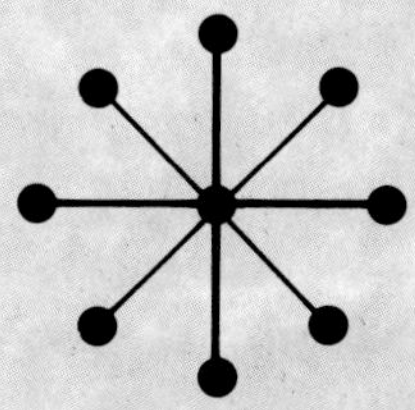

Straight stitches with small beads

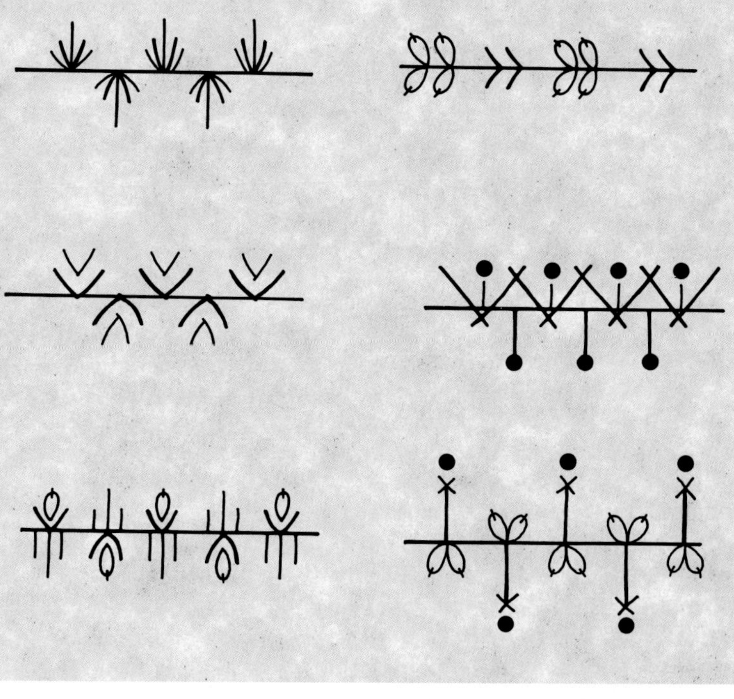

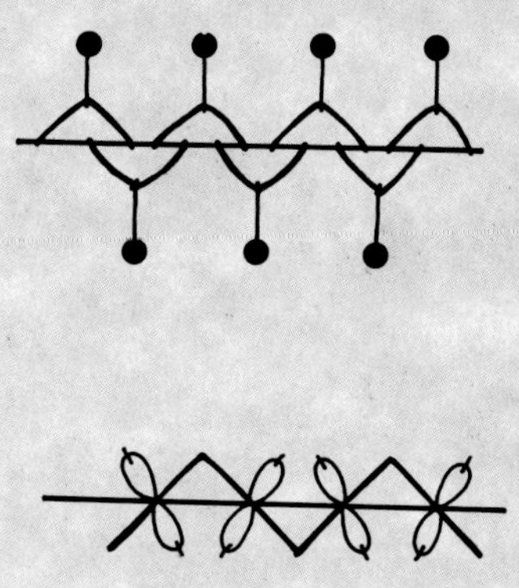

Embroidered Pillow

STITCHED BY FAY KING

The delicate colour of the fabric is reflected in the charming embroidery to create this elegant little pillow.

Materials

- **50 cm (20 in) of grosgrain moiré fabric**
- **DMC stranded thread: Shell Pink 225, Green 3052, Antique Violet 3041, Lemon 745, Blue 800, White, Ecru**
- **straw needles, sizes 8 and 9**
- **Piecemaker tapestry needle**
- **2 m (2¼ yd) of 12 mm (½ in) wide soft silk or rayon ribbon**
- **2 m (2¼ yd) of cord**
- **3 m (3¼ yd) of 4 mm (3/16 in) wide silk ribbon**
- **pencil or water-soluble marker pen**
- **sewing thread for basting**

Method

See the Alphabet on the Pull Out Pattern Sheet.

Embroidery

1 Cut a 30 cm (12 in) square from the fabric. Find the centre of the square by folding the fabric into quarters. Measure and mark points along the folds 10 cm (4 in) from the centre point. Join these points together to make a square. Mark the outline of this square with a line of basting.

2 Carefully pin the rayon ribbon around the marked square, tying a bow at each corner. Where the ribbon ends meet, thread the ends into a tapestry needle and take them through to the back of the work, passing the needle and one end through the other. It is a neater effect if you do this close to one corner. Hold the ribbons and bows in place with French knots, stitched in two strands of Ecru, using the size 8 straw needle.

3 In three corners of the square, embroider a different arrangement of flowers, following the stitch guide on

continued on page 48

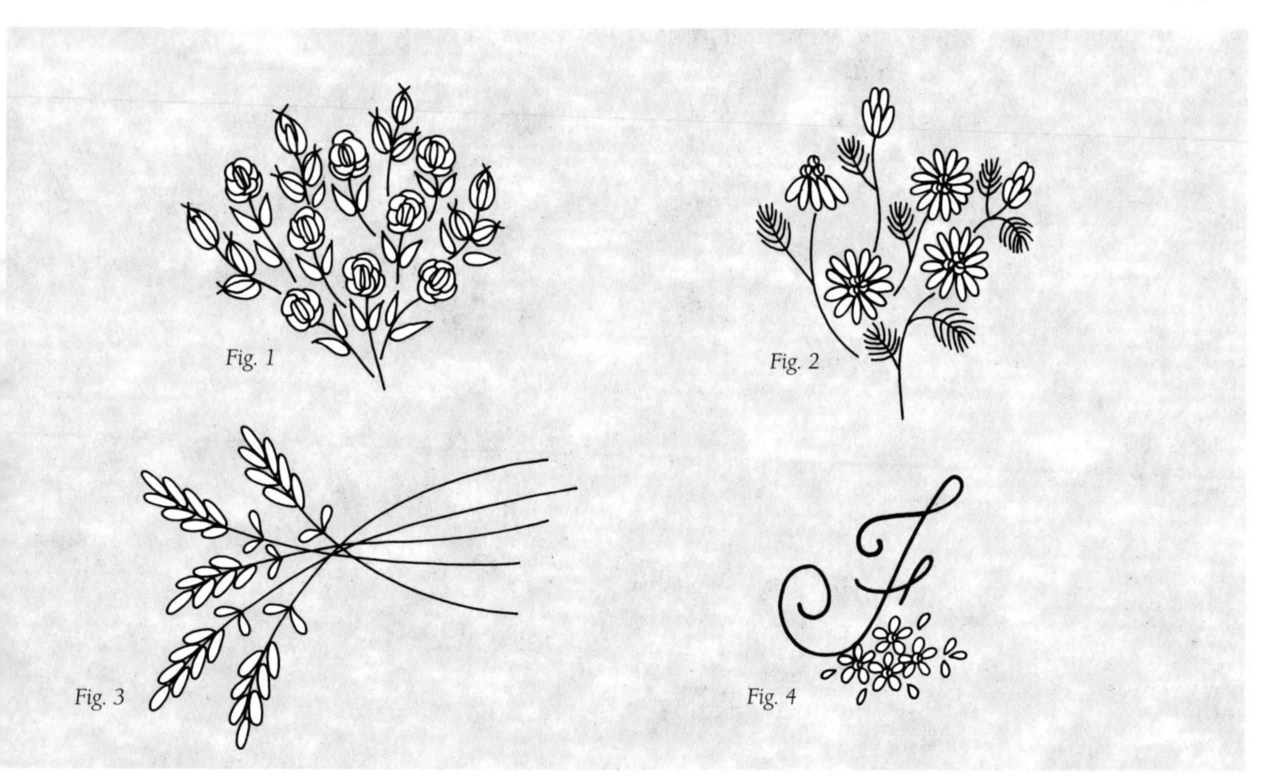

Fig. 1

Fig. 2

Fig. 3

Fig. 4

Stitch Guide

All the roses, lavender and daisies are combinations of bullion stitches worked in appropriate colours. For the bullion stitch instructions, see the stitch guide on page 12.

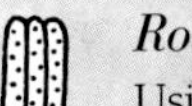

Roses

Using six strands of DMC 225 and a size 3 straw needle, make three bullions side by side for the centre of the rose.

Using six strands of DMC Ecru, make five bullions, working clockwise around the centre and beginning each bullion inside the previous one.

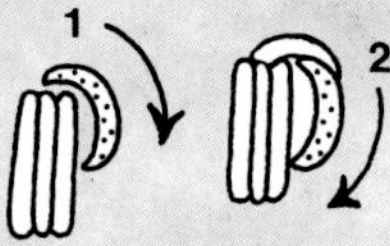

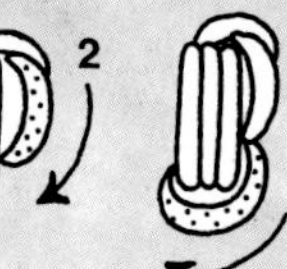

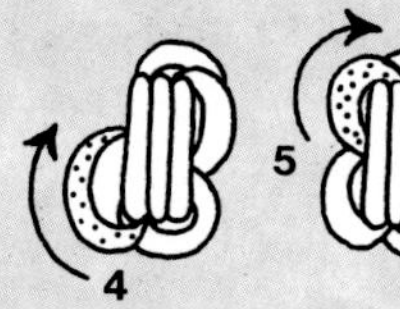

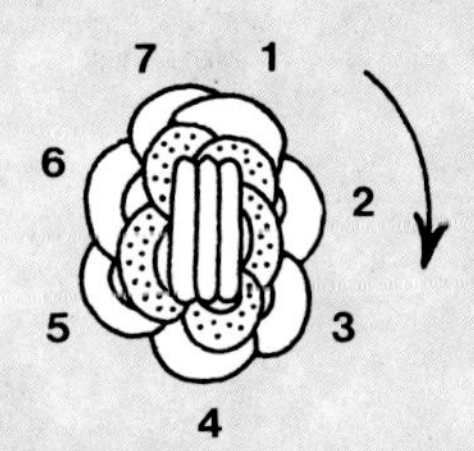

Using six strands of DMC Ecru and a size 3 straw needle, make seven bullions, working clockwise around the centre, in the same way as those made in step 2.

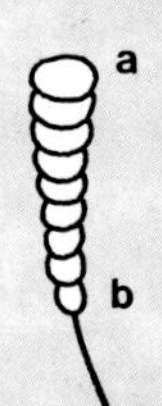

Leaves

Using three strands of DMC 3052 and a size 6 straw needle, make a bullion from **a** to **b** with nine wraps. Ease them off the needle, then give the thread a tug which will tighten the wraps and taper the bullion. Take the needle to the back of your work at **c**.

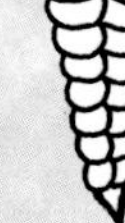

Make a second bullion with eight wraps beside the first one and finish it in the same way.

Small rosebud

Using three strands of DMC 225 and a size 6 straw needle, make one bullion with ten wraps, stitching from **a** to **b**.

Using three strands of DMC Ecru and a size 6 straw needle, make one bullion with twelve wraps on either side of the centre.

Using three strands of DMC 3052 and a size 6 straw needle, make one bullion with fourteen wraps on either side. Tug the thread a little to taper the end. Work three tiny satin stitches across the bottom at **a**.

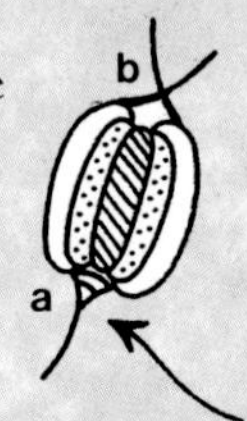

Lavender stems

Work the stems in stem stitch, using two strands of DMC 3052 and a size 8 straw needle.

Gloria's tip: To maintain a graceful curve with stem stitch, always keep the thread to the outside of the curve.

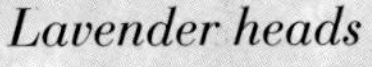
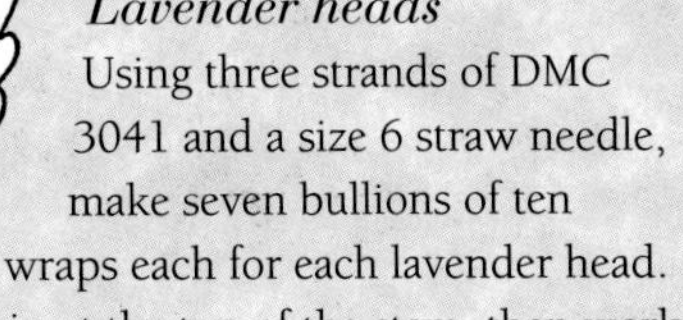

Lavender heads

Using three strands of DMC 3041 and a size 6 straw needle, make seven bullions of ten wraps each for each lavender head. Begin at the top of the stem, then work in the order indicated.

For the bow, bring narrow silk ribbon through from the back of the work and tie a bow at the front.

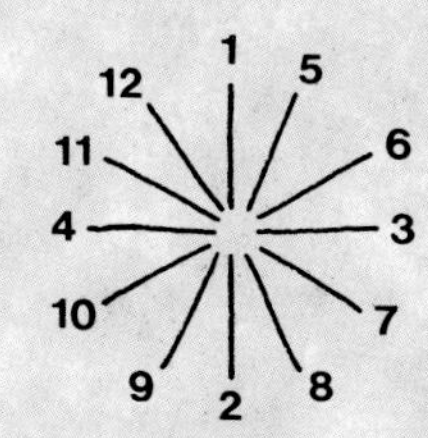

Daisies

Using two strands of DMC Ecru and a size 8 straw needle, make twelve bullions with ten wraps each, working from the centre outwards in the order indicated in the diagram. Position the petals so that there is room for a lemon bullion with six wraps at the centre. Make the bud in the same way, following the diagram on the right.

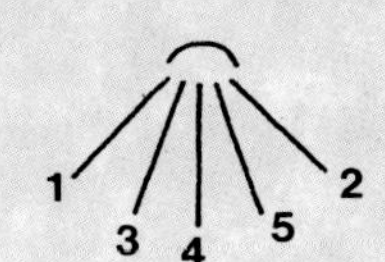

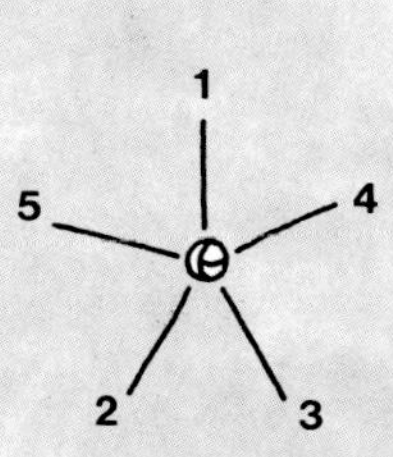

Forget-me-nots

Using three strands of DMC 800 and a size 6 straw needle, make five satin stitch petals in the order indicated on the diagram on the left. For each petal, stitch three or four times from **a** to **b** as shown in the diagram on the right.

Make a French knot in the centre, using two strands of DMC 745 and a size 8 straw needle.

page 46. In the fourth corner, trace the appropriate initial. Stitch the initial in a neat stem stitch, using two strands of embroidery thread. Work over the stem stitch in an even satin stitch, using two strands of thread and the size 8 straw needle. Embroider a spray of forget-me-nots around the initial.

Assembling

1 Cut a second square, 30 cm (12 in), from the fabric. Place this piece and the embroidered piece together with right sides facing. Stitch around 6 mm (1/4 in) from the edge, leaving an opening for turning. Turn the cover to the right side, ensuring that all the corners are neat and square.

2 Beginning at the opening, whipstitch the cord in place around the cover, using matching thread, crossing the cord ends and passing them into the opening. Whipstitch around the cord again – this time with the silk ribbon. Slipstitch the opening closed.

Acknowledgments

With Book Four comes my grateful thanks to everyone who has purchased the first three books.

Many people have had good ideas that turned out not to be so good. I certainly have – otherwise I would be retired and sitting stitching in the shade somewhere. I thought that doing a series of books showcasing the work of Anne's Glory Box was a good idea – and it was!

Thank you Rob James and Judy Poulos from J.B. Fairfax Press for agreeing with me, but, even more importantly, thank YOU all for the 'proof of the pudding' and buying the books. The response, both in Australia and in the United States, has been just wonderful.

All the products shown in this book are available from

Anne's Glory Box
60-62 Beaumont Street
Hamilton, Newcastle, NSW 2303
Phone: (049) 61 6016 or Fax: (049) 61 6587